T0358210

Cambridge Elements ≡

Elements in Histories of Emotions and the Senses
edited by
Rob Boddice
Academy of Finland
Piroska Nagy
Université du Québec à Montréal (UQAM)
Mark Smith
University of South Carolina.

BOREDOM

Elena Carrera
Queen Mary University of London

CAMBRIDGE
UNIVERSITY PRESS

Shaftesbury Road, Cambridge CB2 8EA, United Kingdom

One Liberty Plaza, 20th Floor, New York, NY 10006, USA

477 Williamstown Road, Port Melbourne, VIC 3207, Australia

314–321, 3rd Floor, Plot 3, Splendor Forum, Jasola District Centre, New Delhi – 110025, India

103 Penang Road, #05–06/07, Visioncrest Commercial, Singapore 238467

Cambridge University Press is part of Cambridge University Press & Assessment, a department of the University of Cambridge.

We share the University's mission to contribute to society through the pursuit of education, learning and research at the highest international levels of excellence.

www.cambridge.org
Information on this title: www.cambridge.org/9781009412384

DOI: 10.1017/9781009412360

First published 2023

A catalogue record for this publication is available from the British Library.

ISBN 978-1-009-41238-4 Paperback
ISSN 2632-1068 (online)
ISSN 2632-105X (print)

Boredom

Elements in Histories of Emotions and the Senses

DOI: 10.1017/9781009412360
First published online: August 2023

Elena Carrera
Queen Mary University of London

Author for correspondence: Elena Carrera, e.carrera@qmul.ac.uk

Abstract: This Element challenges prevailing views of boredom as a modern phenomenon and as an experience occurring inside our minds. It discusses the changing perspectives on boredom within psychology, psychiatry and psychoanalysis on both sides of the Atlantic in the last 100 years. It also analyzes visual and textual material from France, Germany, Britain, Argentina and Spain, which illustrates the kinds of social situations, people and interactions that have been considered tedious or boring in the past five centuries. Examining the multidirectional ways in which words like *ennuyeux,* 'tedious', *langweilig, aburrido* and 'boring' have been transferred between different cultural contexts (to denote a range of interrelated feelings that include displeasure, unease and annoyance), it demonstrates how the terms, concepts and categories through which individuals have experienced their states of mind are not simply culture-bound. They have also travelled across geographical and linguistic barriers, through translation, imitation and adaptation. This title is also available as Open Access on Cambridge Core.

Keywords: boredom, intersubjectivity, psychology, visual, cross-cultural history

ISBNs: 9781009412384 (PB), 9781009412360 (OC)
ISSNs: 2632-1068 (online), 2632-105X (print)

Contents

Introduction

'I'm a little bit worried about my safety', she said. 'Mostly, I'm just bored'

(Shih, 2020)

The 'she' in the quotation above is not a female character from a novel written between 1850 and 1930. It is Coco Zhao, a twenty-one-year old student, who was queuing behind hundreds of shoppers at a supermarket in Wuhan at 8.30 am on 27 January 2020. She had spent a few days confined in her hall of residence at Hubei University, playing games on her smartphone, improving her English and 'video-chatting with her parents, who live 60 miles away in another locked-down city in Hubei province' (Shih, 2020). This was less than a week into a quarantine which was predicted to be 'of unprecedented scale', involving fifty-four million people trapped in Wuhan and the densely populated plains around the Yangtze River. As the *Washington Post* China correspondent Gerry Shih pointed out, the people he interviewed in Wuhan were 'beginning to adjust to a surreal reality that could last weeks' (2020). None of us imagined that, less than a month later, Northern Italians would also be living a similarly surreal reality, and so would the rest of us before the end of March. This is the biggest 'us' in the history of civilization. We are too used to understanding ourselves through 'us' and 'them', West and East, women and men, self and other, . . . and now, as I read the word 'bored', an English term that seeks to render to Westerners the feelings of a young Chinese woman, I believe that I understand how she must feel. I believe that Shih, a journalist educated at Columbia University in New York (the son of two academic parents who migrated from Kumming, in southwest China, to the United States before he was born) can convey Zhao's feelings to people with no direct knowledge of Chinese culture. It has been argued that words of emotion are 'actions within relationships' that 'gain their meaning through social cooperation' (Gergen, 2015, p. 98). We are warned that 'researching boredom cross-culturally is fraught with methodological dangers: How can we know what exactly people are experiencing when they say, or we think we see, that they are bored?' (Musharbash, 2007, p. 308). How do we reconcile such caveats with our experience of reading texts in which words evoke feelings, and make us imagine and even feel what we think others must feel?

How many of us think that we know, understand or have a sense of how Zhao must have felt? How many of us glimpse at the photograph in Figure 1 and conclude that the daughter looks bored but the father does not because he seems engaged in whatever he is looking at? The girl might not be bored at all, but simply fed up. Is there an overlap between these feelings? Can we use the term 'boredom' to describe the feelings of people who have never heard that word?

Figure 1 A family looks out from their home on the outskirts
of Wuhan on 27 January. Hector Retamal/AFP/Getty Images

Even if we believe that 'boredom' is a broadly translatable concept, there are
significant cultural differences (see, e.g., Ng *et al.*, 2015), which are best
understood from a historical perspective.

In the spring of 2020, it was not only boredom that hovered over the heads of
millions of school children forced to stay home for months. It was also the
frustration of not being able to move as much or go as far. In Italy and Spain, for
instance, children were not allowed to leave their flats for the best part of eight
weeks, and adults needed a good reason to go out, and could only do so on their
own. According to a March 2020 survey of 3,452 Italians living under national
quarantine, 'boredom' was the second most common complaint, after 'lack of
freedom'. 'Boredom' was ticked more often than 'loneliness', 'lack of social
activities' and the 'loss of job/income source' in the questionnaires (Figure 2).
But one should bear in mind that these were answers to the question 'what are
the main negative sides of complying with the stay home requirement (check all
that apply)?' and that most participants ticked two answers (Barari *et al.*, 2020).
Some respondents might have ticked 'boredom' because doing so produces less
shame than revealing anxieties about job losses or the loss of income. The point
here is that researchers relying on questionnaires need to take into account that
the answers they collect are not simply expressions of feelings, but social acts of
communication, which are shaped by the circumstances in which the answers

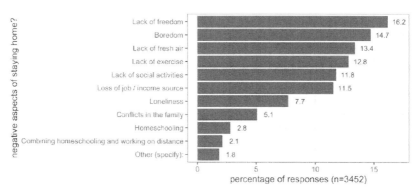

Figure 2 Negative aspects cited by all respondents about staying at home
Source: Barari et al. (2020, p. 8)

are collected, and by the values, expectations and practices that prevail in the respondents' sociocultural milieus.

Of all the survey options, the most difficult to interpret is 'boredom'. Can we assume that the term used in the questionnaire, *noia*, simply means 'boredom'? Like the French *ennui*, the word denotes a broader concept, which encompasses feelings of annoyance, worry, frustration and even impotence, in a situation, perceived as unbearable, from which there seems to be no escape. In this Element, I seek to capture the historical and cross-cultural connotations of the broad concept of boredom in French-, Spanish- and English-speaking contexts since the sixteenth century.

As we will see, the meaning of boredom as an object of study has changed over time, though in the last seventy years it has been shaped (and narrowed down, to a great extent) by the research methods of mainstream psychologists. While in the 1950s psychologists saw boredom as 'a state in which the level of stimulation is perceived as unsatisfactorily low', since the 1980s, boredom has been studied in connection with two extreme situations: deprivation and excess. In a postmodern capitalist culture like ours, in which distractions are commercialized as readily available choices, boredom can be a consequence of sensory and information overload, as the sociologist Georg Simmel warned in 1903. Then came the idea that boredom is an adaptive mechanism, which allows us to switch from less to more relevant stimuli (Klapp, 1986; Blumenberg, 2006; Toohey, 2011; Elpidorou, 2015; Mann, 2016; Danckert and Eastwood, 2020).

Nonetheless, conceptualizing boredom as an adaptive mechanism involves a gross oversimplification of what boredom has meant and the ways it has been experienced in different cultural contexts at different points in history. As Elizabeth Goodstein points out:

Coming to terms with the complexity borne of the historical and cultural shifts in languages of reflection embedded in the experience of boredom calls for more thoughtfully contextualized strategies of definition than an operationalized paradigm can capture. … we must proceed very carefully and critically in developing universalist claims about experience as such that depend on bracketing historical and cultural context. (2020, p. 49)

The universalizing claims of the natural and social sciences, based on the use of single, generic keywords, continue to prevail today despite earlier warnings, like that of the historian of early Europe Edward Peters in 1975, about the need to pay closer attention to the nuanced ways in which language has been used to name, describe and conceptualize experience at different points in history:

Is *boredom* and its roughly cognate terms a useful label for an eternal human emotional state, or should not the question rather be: How did people in the past describe, conceptualize, and perhaps feel what we generically call boredom but must, for historical purposes, study in all its verbal variations and permutations? Surely the under- or overemployed peasant, the seventeenth-century nobleman, aristocratic women, stage-Danish princes, customs-house keepers, and monks did not have identical mental and emotional lives. To retain the generic term *boredom* in studying historical figures and periods is to blur the sometimes fine, sometimes obvious distinctions within societies as well as between historical periods. For the historian, the monk's *acedia,* Hamlet's *melancholia,* Baudelaire's *spleen,* or Oblomov's *lethargy* are not identical emotions, but they are elements of an emotional and social history that is most useful when its particularisms are set off against the generalizing tendencies of the social sciences or the natural sciences. And the key to that differentiation remains, for the time being, in the study of language, semantics, rhetoric, and the visual arts. (1975, pp. 510–11)

Since then, historical approaches to boredom have tended to focus on the 1850s–1920s (Spacks, 1995; Goodstein, 2005; Dalle Pezze and Salzani, 2009; Pease, 2012). There now seems to be a general consensus that 'for a long time in the history of humankind boredom was absent or conceptualized somehow differently as acedia, melancholia, ennui or spleen, which can be interpreted as specific historical modalities of boredom' (Ohlmeier, Finkielsztein and Pfaff, 2020, p. 2012). This view, promoted by a number of non-historians in the last five decades (e.g., Kuhn, 1976; Huguet, 1984; Spacks, 1995; Toohey, 2011; Elpidorou, 2021c; Ros Velasco, 2021, 2022), is clearly reductive as regards pre-modernity, since it only relates to longer-term conditions (like melancholia or ennui), and ignores transient states of mind akin to boredom.

Boredom has been described as 'one of the most socially disvalued, noxious, frequently expressed, and frequently experienced of human emotions', and as 'an extremely unpleasant and distressing experience', typically of 'restlessness combined with lethargy', which can change during people's lifetime (Darden, 1999, p. 14; Martin, Sadlo and Stew, 2006, p. 193; see also Danckert *et al.*, 2018a). But when modern experimental psychologists (writing in English) look back, they tend to look no further than the studies of the physical and mental effects of monotony in the context of modern industry published in English by Hugo Münsterberg (1913) and A. Hudson Davies (1926). At the most, they refer to two types of claims which I problematize in Section 2: that modern boredom dates back to the eighteenth century (Spacks, 1995; Conrad, 1997) and that pre-modern boredom is best understood by looking at discussions of acedia in Late Antiquity and the Middle Ages, and of melancholia in the Renaissance (Toohey, 2011). None of them look at definitions which might capture how boredom was understood before the advent of the term 'boredom', and none of them consider the intersubjective dimension of boredom.

By contrast, I offer here an overview of the longer history of descriptions, discussions and representations of short- and medium-term experiences of boredom, dullness and tediousness. I examine the multidirectional ways in which different terms related to 'boring', like *ennuyeux,* 'tedious', 'dull' and *aburrido,* have travelled between different cultural contexts.

My approach also takes on board the suggestion made by the developmental psychologist Jerome Kagan that we put 'the use of single words' of emotion on hold and 'write about emotional processes with full sentences rather than ambiguous, naked concepts' (2007, p. 216). I take his argument further in two ways. Firstly, by examining how, when people from the past sought to convey their experiences of boredom, weariness or ennui, they utilized the words made available to them, often through texts translated from other languages. Secondly, by drawing on hereto unstudied visual–textual sources.

The few existing studies of boredom which draw on visual material use it to illustrate the discussion of historical textual sources (Toohey, 2011), or they focus completely on modern and contemporary art (Haladyn, 2015). In taking a comparative historical approach, and contrasting modern conceptualizations of boredom with those from pre-industrial societies, I acknowledge some of the creative ways in which boredom has been evoked since the mid-eighteenth century in visual sources in which text is combined with image: satirical prints, caricatures, cartoons and comics. I have chosen such visual sources not only because, as Baudelaire noted when referring to caricatures in 1855, they are the product of a 'perspicacious and bored [*ennuyé*] civilization' (1868, p. 365), but also because they can give us insightful (if often exaggerated) evidence of the types of social interactions that have been considered boring throughout the centuries.[1]

We can see this, for instance, in the cartoon in Figure 3, which might help us reflect on what we ourselves mean by 'boredom', and on the extent to which our own experiences of boredom are shaped by cultural prejudices. Even when boredom seems to be the effect of a particularly asocial situation (as in the isolation caricaturized in Figure 3), it is always social, that is, always situated in a specific historical, cultural and social context, in relation to specific 'emotional styles' (Reddy, 1997) and socially acquired linguistic and emotional repertoires.[2]

Looking at Figure 3, we can also ponder on the reasons why people from the same culture, or even household, who might share an emotional repertoire would disagree with one another on whether it is 'funny', 'witty', 'entertaining', 'boring' or 'none of the above'. The variety of responses one would obtain if one showed it to other people would greatly contrast to the measurable, but rather reductive findings of any questionnaire-based study using those five options.

Figure 3 M J Fry, 'I'm so bored – nothing ever happens around here!'. www
.CartoonStock.com

---

[1] Unless otherwise stated, translations from French, Spanish, Catalan, Italian and German sources
are my own.
[2] For a 'situated' perspective on emotion, see Paul Griffiths and Andrea Scarantino (2009).

Paying attention to various intersubjective aspects of the experience of being bored, I focus on 'boredom' as a multifaceted concept, which denotes a much wider range of feelings, states of mind and communicative acts than can be studied in a lab or through surveys. Building on the valuable insights provided by the existing historical, philosophical, cultural, literary and psychological studies of boredom, as well as on those of journalists and visual (primarily satirical) artists, I take a broad scope and look at a variety of interrelated terms, including 'tediousness' and 'weariness', which, like boredom, could denote both a long-term mood and the effect another person could have on oneself in the short term.

In Section 1, I analyze definitions of boredom and examine the changing perspectives taken by mainstream psychologists since the transfer of experimental methods from Germany to the United States around 1890, placing them against the backdrop of psychiatric and psychoanalytic approaches. I end with a discussion of emotion, language, objectivity and intersubjectivity.

In Section 2, I begin by outlining the methodological approach that I think is best suited to the historical study of emotion, and by examining the exchange-ability of the terms used in Latin, French, English and Spanish before the word 'boredom' came into existence. I then consider textual and (satirical) visual material which discusses, represents or evokes activities normally associated with fun and pleasure, which have also been recognized as potential sources of *fastidium, ennui* or boredom. Crossing linguistic barriers, I seek to demonstrate the importance of early translations of texts originally written in Latin, French and English in Western Europe before 1700, and of the transfer of concepts, social practices, cultural trends and social commentaries between France and Britain in 1750–1820. Then, focusing on Argentina, I briefly discuss some of the transatlantic transfer of people and ideas from Western Europe to America in 1800–1900. I go on to analyze reflections on the experience of *Langeweile* (boredom) in the big modern city in the early twentieth century, and to examine first-, second- and third-person references to boredom in the context of political and social modernization in the Spain of the 1970s–1990s. I finally return to the global context in which researchers of boredom writing in English have posi-tioned themselves in the last few decades.

In examining the kinds of experiences, situations and people designated with terms like *ennuyeux* (and English equivalents like 'tedious') since the sixteenth century, long before the terms 'bore', 'boring' or 'boredom' came into exist-ence, I seek to challenge the supremacy of English keywords in modern scientific approaches to the study of emotion, and to demonstrate the value of taking a cross-cultural (rather than global) approach.

By searching for the meaning of boredom and of related states denoted by complex constellations of terms, such as the English 'weary' and the French *ennuyé,* I also aim to demonstrate how the humanities can move beyond the fragmented realms of academic knowledge by inviting readers to look at 'real life' problems, such as boredom. In reclaiming texts and images as powerful devices for influencing others, I adopt a conciliatory, yet constantly questioning approach, taking the multiple perspectives of a life spent between Scylla and Charybdis, listening to the disconcerting and sometimes nihilistic propositions of postmodernists, social constructivists, philosophical deconstructivists and those who call themselves postfeminists.

In the face of these texts and images, you, readers and viewers, will have the option of remaining unthinking, unengaged, unstimulated or bored. But you might also start to think, feel and reflect in an intersubjective way, with those words and gestures, or against them, putting them on hold, or replacing them with new insights that move you on.

In crossing disciplinary boundaries to find out about other people's experiences and concepts of boredom, weariness and annoyance, you might feel better equipped to understand your own. You will hopefully feel better able to make sense of plurality (without falling into the rabbit hole of relativism), more inclined to repossess language as an ethical and practical tool, readier to challenge the hegemony of the few keywords that have made it to the science of emotion, and more prepared to rethink and reshape its research methods to ensure that experience is not left out of the account.

1 Boredom? What? How?

Boredom seems to have been a widespread complaint well before the Covid-19 confinement exacerbated feelings of boredom around the globe. Those who feel anxious tend to show it. Those who feel lonely might not speak about it; they might have no one to complain to, or might not see the point of doing so. Those who feel bored will probably be saying it loud or in their heads. Boredom is not only a particular kind of 'emotive' (Reddy, 1997, 2001), a feeling we might be aware of when we name it, silently or aloud, with utterances like 'I am bored' or 'this is boring', which shape our experience. 'I am bored' and 'this is boring' can also be calls for help, from those around us who expect us to do something to change the situation that they are finding so tedious. These phrases can, furthermore, resonate in our heads, as an 'alarm', telling us that it is time to move on to another task, another job, another life, even if we do (or can do) nothing about it.

One of the difficulties is that there is no agreement about what constitutes 'boredom'. This is a common problem among social scientists. As Klaus

Scherer has pointed out, social science researchers need to resort to 'everyday language concepts' that are inherently fuzzy and constantly evolving, while also having to move beyond (or ignore) 'inter-language, inter-cultural and inter-individual differences' to be able to define key working concepts in the 'universal, invariant, and consensual fashion generally required by a systematic scientific approach' (2005, p. 696).

1.1 What Is Boredom? Descriptions and Definitions

One main approach to the understanding of the continuum that goes from situational to existential boredom is that of those who blame modern culture for it all and believe that boredom is inescapable (Svendsen, 2005). A second approach locates boredom within the individual, either in distinguishing between ordinary and pathological boredom, as clinical psychologists and psychoanalysts have done, in line with the psychiatrist Henri Le Savoureux (1913, 1914), or in identifying those who are prone to boredom, as experimental psychologists have done since the 1970s. Thirdly, there are those who deny that boredom is a discrete state, or argue that 'one must discriminate and make distinctions when trying to define it. Ennui, apathy, depression, accidie, melancholia, *mal de vivre* —these are all aspects of boredom, but they do not define it' (Epstein, 2012, p. 105). The use of these different labels requires us to make historical, cultural and social distinctions, recognizing, for instance, that the term 'ennui' was adopted by a few English speakers in the eighteenth century to denote a malaise which affected primarily the wealthy idle. Today, the term 'ennui' is not part of the emotional repertoires of the majority of English speakers. The word still carries with it the histories of upper-class sufferers, and has few users, which include historians, literary scholars and middle-aged cartoon characters like that in Figure 4. As a keyword, it can serve to distinguish the long-term anguished boredom associated with privileged existentialists from the fleeting state of boredom (even though it is not always possible to differentiate between them).

One of the broadest perspectives on boredom is that provided by the behavioural scientist Dennis Brissett and sociologist Robert Snow. Elaborating on Colin Wilson's definition of boredom as 'being stuck in the present' (1972, p. 255), they explain it as 'the experience of "dead ending," of being someplace with nowhere to go, of being disengaged from the ebb and flow of human interaction', which occurs 'when what is going on has no, or too few, personally viable implications for the future of the bored person' (1993, pp. 240–1).

Few contemporary definitions of boredom refer to feelings of irritability or annoyance. The sociologist Jack Barbalet describes boredom as the 'restless,

"The crushing boredom has became somehow
ennobled since I started calling it ennui."

Figure 4 Chris Wildt, 'The crushing boredom has become somehow
ennobled since I started calling it ennui'. www.CartoonStock.com

irritable feeling' of not being involved or engaged in a current activity or
situation which 'holds no appeal', and needing 'to get on with something
interesting' (1999, pp. 631, 634–5). Among medical researchers, Michael
Spaeth and his colleagues focus on 'leisure boredom' (as opposed to boredom
at school or at work) and define it as 'the subjective core impression that there is
nothing meaningful to do and that the time is passing slowly, accompanied by
feelings of dissatisfaction, despondency, annoyance, stress, and a sense of
entrapment' (2015, p. 1380).

The definitions offered by psychologists allow us, in principle, to see boredom as a spectrum or continuum of mental states, which can be short, medium
or long term. Some have emphasized that it is a form of rejection, alongside
disgust, loathing, dislike and tiresomeness (Plutchik, 1962). Others have suggested that 'boredom is the experience of being disengaged from the world and
stuck in a seemingly endless and dissatisfying present', and that its central
feature is the 'aversive experience of wanting, but being unable, to engage in
stimulating and satisfying activity' (Fahlman *et al.*, 2013, pp. 68–9). Boredom
can thus be broadly defined in psychological terms as the aversive state of an
individual who is unable to pay attention to information from internal or
external sources (feelings and thoughts, or stimuli) necessary to participate in
a satisfying activity. Those experimental psychologists who focus on short-term
states which can be induced, measured and compared readily emphasize the

element of transience: 'boredom is an unpleasant, transient affective state in which the individual feels a pervasive lack of interest in and difficulty concentrating on the current activity' (Fisher, 1993, p. 396; see also Eastwood *et al.*, 2012).

By contrast, philosophers have tended to emphasize the sense of emptiness associated with boredom. For instance, in 1818, Schopenhauer described life as swinging 'like a pendulum' between suffering and boredom (1969, p. 312). In his view, 'happiness and well-being' was to only be found in 'the transition from desire to satisfaction, and from this to a fresh desire', and thus people experienced the absence of satisfaction as 'suffering' and the 'empty longing for a new desire' as 'languor, boredom' (p. 260). This is the approach taken by the novelist Tolstoy, who defined tedium in *Anna Karenina* (in 1877) as 'the desire for desires' (2016, p. 467).

While Schopenhauer located emptiness within the bored individual, the philosopher and psychologist William James described boredom as an experience of 'empty time':

> *Taedium, ennui, Langweile,* boredom, are words for which, probably, every language known to man has its equivalent. It comes about whenever, from the relative emptiness of content of a tract of time, we grow attentive to the passage of the time itself. Expecting, and being ready for, a new impression to succeed; when it fails to come, we get an empty time instead of it; and such experiences, ceaselessly renewed, make us most formidably aware of the extent of the mere time itself. (1886, p. 392)

Speaking of boredom as seemingly universal phenomenon, and a widely translatable concept, James defined it in passing as the 'odiousness of time that seems long from its emptiness' and explained that 'the odiousness of the whole experience comes from its insipidity' (p. 392). His understanding of boredom encompassed both the slowness of time denoted by the German term *Langeweile* and the sense of aversion evoked by the French *ennui* (derived from the Late Latin *inodiare,* 'to cause aversion, to make hateful'). He believed that 'stimulation is the indispensable requisite for pleasure in an experience, and the feeling of bare time is the least stimulating experience we can have' (p. 392), Thus, from his perspective, boredom arises from the unfulfilled expectation that time should be spent in stimulating ways.

The earlier notion of empty longing gained new prominence among psychoanalysts, who have invariably focused on boredom as a longer-term state. Among them, Ralph Greenson offered one of the most comprehensive descriptions:

> The uniqueness of the feeling of being bored seems to depend upon the coexistence of the following components: a state of dissatisfaction and a disinclination to action; a state of longing and an inability to designate

> what is longed for; a sense of emptiness; a passive, expectant attitude with the
> hope that the external world will supply the satisfaction; a distorted sense of
> time in which time seems to stand still. (1953, p. 7)

Similarly, Adam Phillips has stressed that boredom is always accompanied by 'that most absurd and paradoxical wish, the wish for a desire', though he has also pointed out that it encompasses a 'multiplicity of moods and feelings that resist analysis' (1993, p. 78). This latter observation can be related to the claims about the 'infinite plasticity' and 'unbridled polymorphism' of boredom (*ennui*) made by Émile Tardieu at the *fin-de-siècle* (1900, p. 1).

Long-term boredom has also been explained as an existential sense of emptiness arising from the more or less conscious realization that most pursuits are futile, and therefore meaningless. Thus, the philosopher of religion Michael Raposa suggests that 'the bored person has plenty of nothing' (1999, p. 45). Seeing boredom as 'an experience (however dimly understood as such) of the emptiness that lurks at the heart of human existence, an emptiness into which each moment fades, into which all finite things pass away', he claims that 'boredom itself represents the death of meaning, of interest' (1999, p. 60).

In turn, cultural critics have tended to conclude that, despite their efforts, 'there can be no exact or meticulous definition for boredom' (Paliwoda, 2010, p. 2). Some describe boredom as a 'vague disquiet' (Kuhn, 1976, p. 9) or as a 'vaguely disquieting mood' (Goodstein, 2005, p. 18), while acknowledging that this can take many shapes. Others argue that boredom can only be evoked through metaphors, such as that suggested by Brodsky: 'the psychological Sahara that starts in your bedroom' (1995, p. 110). Yet others suggest that boredom is 'not easily dissected and contained', and that attempting to classify it by making lexical distinctions would be reductive:

> Given the rather complex nature of boredom, to splinter it into disparate
> notions and bewildering lexicon and to insist on rigid constructs and abstruse
> diagnoses is to deny, constrict, and blunt its restless and existential complex-
> ion. Boredom is a force in its tidal-like action against the self: it ebbs and
> flows .... Boredom may vary in its strength and duration, but is an unified,
> although complicated, existential state .... In its most basic sense, boredom
> is the decisive point in ... consciousness when meaning is eroded; the
> absence or destruction of meaning, whether it be short-lived or sustained.
> (Paliwoda, 2010, p. 2)

The absence of meaning seems an important part of the experience of boredom, though it is more difficult to measure than the absence of stimulation.

In *Existentialism* (1947), Sartre suggested that, since life has no a priori meaning, and since it is up to individuals to create meaning in their lives, bored people are those who expect others to make their lives meaningful.

More recently, the philosopher Lars Svendsen has pointed out that meaning is not out there or inside oneself, but in one's relation to the world:

> Boredom involves a loss of meaning, and a loss of meaning is serious for the afflicted person. I do not believe that we can say that the world appears to be meaningless because one is bored, or that one is bored because the world appears to be meaningless. There is hardly a simple relationship here between a cause and an effect. But boredom and a loss of meaning are connected. (2005, p. 17)

Sartre's and Svendsen's arguments, as I shall try to demonstrate, can be taken further by exploring the intersubjective connections that have been part of meaning-making, and the disconnectedness that appears to be at the root of boredom in much of its historical occurrence.

1.2 Changing 'Psy-Science' Perspectives: 100 Years of Experiments on Boredom

For the last 100 years, it has been recognized that boredom is disagreeable and distressing, and that it has a negative impact on the quality of an individual's work (Davies, 1926; Thackray, 1981). A great deal of the research on boredom conducted by psychologists has been based on the 'experimental' methods (measurement, quantification and statistics) developed by German psychologists around the mid-nineteenth century. These methods, which consisted in obtaining introspective data and 'eliminating their uncertainty by operating on a large scale and taking statistical means', were described by James in *The Principles of Psychology* as 'a microscopic psychology' (1890, p. 192). He suggested that this type of research was too boring for non-Germans:

> This method taxes patience to the utmost, and could hardly have arisen in a country whose natives could be bored. Such Germans as Weber, Fechner, Vierordt, and Wundt obviously cannot; and their success has brought into the field an array of younger experimental psychologists, bent on studying the elements of the mental life, dissecting them out from the gross results in which they are embedded, and as far as possible reducing them to quantitative scales. The simple and open method of attack having done what it can, the method of patience, starving out, and harassing to death is tried; the Mind must submit to a regular siege, in which minute advantages gained night and day by the forces that hem her in must sum themselves up at last into her overthrow. There is little of the grand style about these new prism, pendulum, and chronograph-philosophers. They mean business, not chivalry. (1890, pp. 192–3)

In line with his understanding of boredom as resulting from a lack of stimulation, James believed that the 'minute' tasks of experimenters were boring because they did not yield significant results in themselves, but only after many small, time-consuming steps had been taken.

Four years later, Ernst Meumann published the results of an experimental study on the link between physical fatigue and boredom conducted at Wilhelm Wundt's Institute of Experimental Psychology in Leipzig (1894). The alienating effects of mechanization and the division of labour also became the focus of the attention of the trained physician Hugo Münsterberg, who had completed his PhD in experimental psychology under Wundt's supervision in 1885, and obtained a chair at Harvard in 1897 with James's help. In his highly influential *Psychology and Industrial Efficiency* (1913), based on a series of lectures he had given at the University of Berlin in 1910–1911, Münsterberg defined 'monotony' as the 'subjective dislike of uniformity' (cited in Campbell, 1989, p. 77). Drawing on Münsterberg, Davies employed the term 'monotony' in the title of his study in the context of British Industry (1926), though he used it interchangeably with 'boredom'.

Following this line of inquiry, in the 1920s–1950s, psychologists' research on boredom focused primarily on industrial settings, using a combination of observation and interviews, and reaching conclusions which took account of individual differences in age and level of education (e.g., Smith, 1942). Other studies of fatigue and boredom at work included one on their effects on teachers' marks (Dexter, 1935). Meanwhile, French psychiatrists continued to study pathological boredom (*ennui morbide*), drawing on Le Savoureux (1913, 1914), as well as on early nineteenth-century medical and philosophical ideas, such as Maine de Biran's explanation of *ennui* as the result of 'a general need of excitement that has not been satisfied' (cited in Dupuis, 1922, p. 419). Deep *ennui,* seen as a mental illness, was characterized by the loss of desire and interest, caused either by the sustained failure to satisfy previous desires or by the satisfaction of all desires (Benon, 1939).

In the 1930s–1970s, psychoanalysts focused on boredom as an inability consciously to determine what is desired, and explained this as the result of the repression of a threatening desire. As Otto Fenichel put it in 1934, boredom 'arises when we must not do what we want to do, or must do what we do not want to do' (1951, p. 359, see also 1953; Greenson, 1953; Wangh, 1975). Hilde Lewinsky (1907–1956), who fled Nazi Germany, went to Paris, and settled in Manchester in 1934 and in New York in 1951, stressed the idea that boredom was a social problem which manifested itself both at work and in the context of leisure. Boredom, in her view, was best defined in the terms suggested by Theodor Lipps in *Leitfaden der Psychologie* (Guide to Psychology, 1903): 'a feeling of displeasure due to the conflict between the urge for intense psychic occupation and the lack of stimulation or the incapacity to allow oneself to be stimulated' (Lewinsky, 1943, pp. 147–48). As she explained, Fenichel (whose work had not yet been published in English) had drawn on Lipps, but also observed that, in cases of pathological boredom, 'the urge for intense psychic occupation' tends to be accompanied by an 'inhibition of doing anything' and a sense of not knowing what to do; in such cases, the tension produced by 'impulse stimulation' is felt, but the aim of this impulse remains unconscious, having been 'repressed because it is not socially acceptable' (Lewinsky, 1943, p. 148). Clarifying that the fear of 'being alone and/or without occupation' was usually the manifestation of the fear of boredom (rather than boredom itself), Lewinsky went as far as suggesting that people who tended to get bored could avoid boredom if they 'allow[ed] themselves a certain freedom of phantasy [i.e., imagination]' (p. 148). She also pointed out that what was usually thought of as 'boredom' in healthy individuals were often reactions of 'impatience and anger' at being forced to do things which did not stimulate interest and pleasure (p. 148).

Ten years later, Heinrich Racker, a Polish–Argentinian psychoanalyst of Austrian-Jewish origin, gave a paper on transference and countertransference at the Argentinian Association of Psychoanalysists, in which he drew attention to the analyst's boredom in response to the patient's emotional withdrawal. Racker's ensuing publication (in English) became a landmark (1957, reprinted 2007), but his findings about the intersubjective dimension of boredom have only recently begun to attract the attention they deserve (e.g., Palerm, 2016).

As for experimental psychologists, a shift took place in 1960, when the new focus was the mismatch between an individual's need for arousal and the availability of environmental stimulation, such as the degree of challenge, complexity, intensity and variety (Berlyne, 1960; Hebb, 1966; Csikszentmihalyi, 1975, 1997; Zuckerman, 1979; Klapp, 1986; de Chenne, 1988). It was recognized that boredom could be accompanied by conflict and frustration: 'when attempts to escape from the situation are thwarted by social pressure or other obstacles, conflict and frustration can be expected to push arousal still higher' (Berlyne, 1960, p. 191).

By the late 1970s, boredom had begun to form part of a larger picture, as some scholars turned their attention to ongoing feelings such as 'dissatisfaction with life', the relationship between boredom and addictive behaviours, such as overeating, and the link between proneness to boredom and physical complaints (Abramson and Stinson, 1977; Sommers and Vodanovich, 2000; Crockett, Myhre and Rokke, 2015; Moynihan *et al.*, 2015). Since then, psychological studies of boredom have tended to focus on measuring (e.g., seeking to establish causal links between boredom and low academic achievement), individual differences (proneness to boredom as a trait) and mental health.

The most comprehensive tool for measuring boredom to date is the Boredom Proneness Scale, a twenty-eight-item self-report measure created by Farmer and Sundberg (1986). Others include the Boredom Susceptibility Scale (a ten-item subscale of Zuckerman's (1979) Sensation Seeking Scale), the Boredom Coping Scale (Hamilton, Haier and Buchsbaum, 1984), the Job Boredom Scale (Lee, 1986), the Leisure Boredom Scale (Iso-Ahola and Weissinger, 1990), the Free Time Boredom Scale (Ragheb and Merydith, 2001) and the Sexual Boredom Scale (Watt and Ewing, 1996). Nevertheless, it can be argued that, since the questionnaires used in such psychometric tools rely on introspective answers, they are of limited value in the study of boredom because people who tend to experience bouts of boredom have been found to have low emotional awareness – namely, a limited ability to identify, describe and label emotions accurately (Bernstein, 1975; Harris, 2000; Eastwood *et al.*, 2007; Mercer-Lynn *et al.*, 2013a; Mercer-Lynn, Hunter and Eastwood, 2013b). How can researchers of boredom quantify the introspective questionnaire answers of people who might be too bored to know that they are bored?

In the twenty-first century, experimental psychological research on boredom has grown exponentially and included an increasingly wide range of situations and social settings (Vodanovich, 2003; Vodanovich and Watt, 2016).[3] However, while researchers continue to distinguish between boredom as a disposition or trait and as a state, the existing methods for measuring the latter are still rather limited. For instance, the twenty-nine items of the Multidimensional State Boredom Scale designed by Shelley Fahlman and her colleagues (2013) can be grouped into five areas: disengagement, high arousal (agitation), inattention, low arousal and the feeling that time is passing slowly. But only seven of these items can reliably distinguish bored from non-bored people (Hunter *et al.*, 2016). It has also been found that a multi-item scale produces similar expressions of boredom as single-item measures like 'I feel bored' (Markey *et al.*, 2014).

In the last ten years, renewed emphasis has been placed on the negative aspects of boredom and addiction (particularly drug abuse), but boredom has also been studied as a gateway to creativity (e.g., Mann and Cadman, 2014), as well as in relation to particular occupations and, more generally, to well-being at work (e.g., boredom as a factor of burnout). In exploring further the association between boredom and compulsive behaviours such as substance use, gambling and self-harm, some studies have sought to redefine what we

---

[3] A search of the PsycINFO database using the term 'boredom' as keyword in late August 2020 yielded a total of 3,186 citations, four times the number given in Vodanovich and Watt (2016) for 2015 and 200 times their number for 2005.

mean by boredom (e.g., Mercer and Eastwood, 2010). Since boredom is not just one phenomenon (even if it is often seen in broad terms as a 'modern phenomenon'), psychologists would benefit from considering the more nuanced understandings of boredom that can be gained from other disciplines and methods, such as philosophy, sociology, history and textual and visual analysis.

1.3 Emotion, Language and Intersubjectivity

Knowing how we feel is not a lone act. Experience is not a private event, located inside the individual. If it were, we would not be able to use words to make it intelligible to other people, as Wittgenstein pointed out (1958; see Overgaard, 2006). There is thus no reason to believe, as Andrew Ortony, Gerald Clore and Allan Collins seem to do (1988), that individuals cannot be mistaken about their experiences. The assumption that individuals have privileged access to their own experience is simply part of the Cartesian legacy (Mascolo and Kallio, 2020).

As Peter Hacker has noted, the earliest physiological psychologists, like Wundt, 'attempted to relate mental events and processes to neural and cortical processes', based on a Cartesian and Lockean conception of the mind, and they took for granted that introspection was 'akin to a faculty of sense by the exercise of which each person is able to report (fallibly or infallibly) on mental events, states and processes, which can then be correlated with neural ones' (2012, p. 211). James, who had a crucial role in introducing experimental psychology to the United States, defined 'introspection' as 'looking into one's own mind and reporting what we there discover', and assumed that 'everyone agrees that we there discover states of consciousness' (1890, p. 185). This perspective was challenged by Wittgenstein, who disputed the idea of 'privileged access to the mind and its contents – as if each of us had access to a private peepshow'– and the belief 'that the study of psychology is unavoidably secondhand – that a subject sees what passes in his own mind, and reports it to the psychologist' (Hacker, 2012, p. 212). He also questioned the idea that emotions are inside the individual:

> "We see emotion." – As opposed to what? – We do not see facial contortions and make the inference that he is feeling joy, grief, boredom. We describe a face immediately as sad, radiant, bored, even when we are unable to give any other description of the features. ... In general I do not surmise fear in him – I see it. I do not feel that I am deducing the probable existence of something inside from something outside; rather, it is as if the human face were in a way translucent and that I were seeing it not in reflected light but rather in its own. (Wittgenstein, 1980, p. 170)

Expression, for Wittgenstein, is the public manifestation of experience, not separate from it. He did not see experience as an 'a priori hidden phenomenon' that precedes behaviour, but argued that experience is always embodied and that 'expression' is part of 'embodied experience' (Mascolo, 2009, p. 265). The psychologist Paul Ekman agrees with this view in as far as he argues that 'expression is a central feature of emotion, not simply an outer manifestation of an internal phenomena' (1993, p. 384). But, while Wittgenstein paid attention to language, Ekman does not.

Wittgenstein emphasized how children learn to express and identify emotions intersubjectively, even before they acquire language, through social interactions in which emotions are expressed and named. As Michael Mascolo puts it in a study that shows the relevance of Witgenstein's approach to the discursive analysis of emotion:

> By the time that they begin to acquire language, children have already gained a richly inter-subjective (although pre-reflective) appreciation of the emotional life of self and other. Children acquire the capacity to play the language game of identifying emotions in others by learning to use emotion words that have their consensual basis in public expressions of emotion. In this way, everyday emotion concepts specify public criteria for the identification of emotions in others. (2009, p. 265)

As Mascolo further explains, individuals identify emotion in others through 'dialectical interplay', which 'begins with using everyday emotion words to make intuitive, pre-reflective classification' and often continues with a 'process of reflecting upon and making explicit the public criteria that mediate such implicit pre-reflective judgments' (p. 265). Identifying one's own emotion through introspection involves 'secondary (and higher-order) acts of reflection that are mediated by the available emotion lexicon'; it is never the result of a 'transparent access to a private emotional state' (p. 266).

Thus, from Wittgenstein's perspective, the utterance 'I am bored' is an expression of a person's emotional state, rather than a description of the experience of being bored. Human language does not simply name emotions; it mediates and expresses emotion in more nuanced ways than can be expressed by sentient beings (like animals and babies) who do not use language. As Hacker has pointed out, 'to learn a language is to learn new forms of behaviour and action, of social interaction and response' (2012, p. 207). Harry Smit has expanded on this idea, noting that it is through language that we learn communicative behaviour: to 'demand, beg and request; to call people and to respond to calls; to express needs, sensations and emotions and to respond to the expressions of others; to ask and answer questions; to name things and to describe and to respond to descriptions of how things are' (2014, p. 158). The emergence of language in the evolution of the human species led to the 'extension and replacement of behavior already displayed by our predecessors'; it allowed complex forms of communicative behaviour, including 'expressions of intending, thinking and imagining' (pp. 158–9).

This perspective on language and psychology was put forward by Wittgenstein in the late 1940s in a work which has been available in English since 1980, but has had little bearing on the questionnaire-based psychological study of boredom. Can psychologists know how people feel if all they get from them are standard, measurable questionnaire answers about some standardized feeling categorized as 'boredom'?

In 1954, Alfred Schutz pointed out,

> alluding to a statement Kant made in another context, that it [was] a "scandal of philosophy" that so far the problem of our knowledge of other minds and, in connection therewith, of the intersubjectivity of our experience of the natural as well as the socio-cultural world, ha[d] not found a satisfactory solution and that, until rather recent times, this problem ha[d] even escaped the attention of philosophers. (1954, p. 265)

At that time (and now), 'all forms of naturalism and logical empiricism simply [took] for granted this social reality, which is the proper object of the social sciences. Intersubjectivity, interaction, intercommunication, and language [were] simply presupposed as the unclarified foundation of these theories' (p. 261). If, in the 1950s, intersubjectivity was 'simply presupposed as the unclarified foundation of the explanatory-empirical sciences' (Percy, 1958, p. 631), to what extent is it even presupposed today?

The term 'intersubjectivity' was redeployed by Jürgen Habermas as an alternative to the traditional epistemological approaches which base truth and meaning on empirical observation or on individual consciousness. As he noted, human knowledge is not restricted to empirically testable hypotheses arrived at through disinterested, value-free inquiry, of the kind which the positivists believed they were capable of. Nor can knowledge be reduced to insights produced in individual minds, since insights have no value unless they are communicated in accessible terms, in well-reasoned discourse.

Rejecting both positivist naturalism and classical hermeneutics, Habermas argued that, in the sciences, as in the humanities, objectivity can only be attained through 'intersubjective agreement', or the rational, negotiated assent among autonomous responsible individuals. The sphere of intersubjectivity is that of 'mutual understanding': a capacity that surpasses any one individual and is exercised in the social domain through socialization, and primarily through language acquisition (1984). This 'mutual understanding' involves successful acts of communication, which necessarily rely on four (intersubjective) validity claims: comprehensibility (the use of comprehensible expressions, which both speaker and listener understand), truth (the use of empirical propositions believed to be factually valid), truthfulness or sincerity (shared intentions that elicit the reciprocal trust necessary for openness and self-disclosure) and appropriateness (tone, pitch of voice and expressions, which are fitting to the relationship between speaker and listener) (1984). Such claims imply an ideal interaction (and context) undistorted by domination, ignorance, violence or coercion.

Mutual understanding is not always present in everyday verbal interactions. Nor has it been sufficiently pursued across the epistemological and methodological boundaries that keep the humanities, the life sciences and the social sciences in separate fields of action. We have seen how, in the last 100 years, some researchers in the social sciences (like Davies, May Smith and other early industrial psychologists) sought to take account of the impact on the experience of boredom of factors such as social class, age, gender and level of education. By contrast, those who have taken a scientific approach to the emotions in recent years have focused on keywords such as 'boredom' to facilitate comprehensibility, on measures such as 'arousal' to attain empirical validity, and on statistical methods to translate introspective questionnaire answers into objective data. I will now turn to the humanities to explore how people's experiences of boredom in the past were shaped by their expectations, their social interactions, their power relations, the situations in which they found themselves (out of necessity or following the latest fashion) and the nuances of the language available to them.

2 What Has Been Boring, Tedious and *Ennuyeux* in the Last 500 Years?

Throughout the ages, boredom has been experienced in relation to potentially pleasant activities (like learning), or artefacts (like cartoons). In 1854, Paolo Mantegazza (1831–1910), a pioneer in social hygiene, noted in his *Fisiologia del piacere* (Physiology of Pleasure) that 'the pleasures of learning vary in an endless scale depending on the subject. Those who are particularly keen on Maths might yawn when reading a History book; the linguist might remain indifferent when listening to the most interesting Chemistry lecture and so on' (1867, p. 422). There is nonetheless a huge difference between acknowledging that what pleases one academic bores another, and making claims such as that recently made by the PhD student Amir Baghdadchi: 'the kind of boredom experienced in academia is unique' (2005, p. 319). The example Baghdadchi gives, that the most interesting paper given at a conference of English scholars might bore those attending an engineering conference, and vice versa, is similar to Mantegazza's observation. But he also argues that the boredom we might experience in a seminar is not simply a subjective state or feeling, and that what makes academic papers and seminars boring is the emphasis on rigour, rather than usefulness. The line that separates the 'boring' from the 'merely interesting' is highly subjective, and can be the object of academic debate (Ngai, 2008), though there is also something to be said about the capacity of certain speakers and writers to engage audiences beyond their discipline.

Most of us would agree that 'boring' is neither a fully subjective experience nor an objective quality. Toohey suggests in passing that boredom can be differentiated from melancholy in that it 'is a social emotion and it looks outward at a confining or monotonous situation' (2011, p. 35). What scholars have failed to notice is that boredom can also be an intersubjective experience, not only when it is perceived to be caused by another person, but also in as far as it is shaped, communicated and identified through language.

In the past, privileged people who were able to read (and had the leisure to do so) often resorted to reading (or being read to) as a way of changing their mood when they were in low spirits, bored or *ennuyés*. For instance, a late nineteenth-century dictionary suggests that 'reading chases boredom away [*la lecture désennuye*]'. The other traditional way of chasing boredom away noted in the dictionary is 'to play [*jouer*]', exemplified with the following lines from the popular medieval air, *Chanson du comte Ory:* 'The count Ory used to say for fun/that he wanted to take the convent Farmoutier/ to be able to please the nuns and chase away his *ennui*' (Littré, 1863, s.v. 'désennuyer').

Unlike reading, talking playfully about illicit desires and fantasizing about transgressive sex has never been restricted to the literate upper classes. Littré chose this example to show that the term *désennuyer* existed since the Middle Ages, but this did not restrict the meaning of playfulness and play as antidotes to *ennui*. The French even had a noun, *chasse-ennui,* to convey the idea of dispelling *ennui*. For centuries, the term *ennui* denoted a range of heavy feelings, which included sadness and worry, as well as what we now call 'boredom', and the term *chasse-ennui* denoted activities like reading or listening to entertaining stories, watching plays, laughing with friends and being playful. These activities were considered essential ways of preserving one's physical and mental health in the Hippocratic approach to medicine which prevailed (under names like 'regimens of health' and 'hygienic medicine') until the early twentieth century. The English language did not have a specific term for *chasse-ennui,* but early modern French–English dictionaries offered translations like 'cheering up' and 'care-expelling' (Cotgrave, 1611, s.v. 'chasse-ennui').

In the most influential cultural history of boredom to date, Patricia Spacks has suggested that 'if people felt bored before the late eighteenth century, they didn't know it', that boredom appeared in that century as 'a new concept, if not necessarily a new event', that it allowed new ways of understanding the world to be articulated, and that it 'has haunted Western society ever since its eighteenth-century invention' (1995, pp. 28, 272). It is understandable that, as an expert on the eighteenth century, Spacks did not look at references to experiences akin to boredom, such as 'tedious-ness', 'weariness' and their sixteenth- and seventeenth-century variants. These, as we shall see in this section, suggest that, in the eighteenth century, there was no clear break with the concepts denoted by the French term *ennui* and by the English terms used to translate it in earlier centuries. Yet Spacks's claims have been often quoted by historians like Susan Matt (Fernandez and Matt, 2019), as well as by literary scholars, sociologists and psychologists, who perpetuate the erroneous belief that the English term 'boredom' captures a single concept, invented in the eight-eenth century.

The concept of boredom that Spacks locates in the eighteenth century was surely broader than the use of words like 'bore' and 'boring', which only appeared late in the century and only did so among a few members of the upper classes in very limited geographical areas, like parts of London, Oxford and Bath. The noun 'bore' (or rather, the variant 'boar') is attested in a letter by Lady Sarah Lennox dated 9 January 1766 (1901, p. 179). According to Francis Grose's *Classical Dictionary of the Vulgar Tongue,* 'bore' became a fashionable word in 1780–1781, and was used to refer to 'a tedious, troublesome man or woman, one who bores the ears of his listeners with an uninteresting tale' (1785, s.v. 'bore').

There are three main considerations here. Firstly, given that the noun 'bore' has been used since the late 1760s to refer to 'tiresome people and conversa-tions' (*OED*, 2020, s.v. 'bore', v.2), it is surprising that no scholar has yet considered boredom as an 'intersubjective' experience. Secondly, in writing the history of a particular emotion (or state of mind), one needs to go beyond the history of a single word. Thirdly, one needs to acknowledge that the fact that a word, like 'bore', existed in English does not mean that people used it much. It took another 100 years for the term 'bore' to be more broadly used, and even then, it appears to have been unknown in much of England. This can be gathered, for instance, from the unfamiliarity with the term shown in the late nineteenth century by a character in Thomas Hardy's *The Hand of Ethelberta*. Having just arrived in London, Ethelberta's sister does not know 'town words' and thus does not understand the term 'bore' when she hears their brother use it to refer to her receiving many visitors (Hardy, 1876, p. 136).

In any case, as Samuel Johnson suggested in an essay published in *The Adventurer* on 2 October 1753, very little of what his contemporaries claimed as a novelty was actually new:

> It is often charged upon writers, that with all their pretensions to genius and discoveries, they do little more than copy one another; and that compositions obtruded upon the world with the pomp of novelty, contain only tedious repetitions of common sentiments, or at best exhibit a transposition of known images, and give a new appearance to truth only by some slight difference of dress and decoration. (1834, p. 334)

Excessive repetition, as we shall see, can make the most pleasant experiences 'tedious', and can have a dulling effect on the mind. Novelty, by contrast, can create interest, but only, as Johnson suggests, when it is not limited to appearances. The educated among Johnson's contemporaries were drawing on ideas and 'sentiments' expressed in other languages, like Latin and French, only to find that the basic concepts of the new French culture were built on principles and ideas already promoted in Ancient Rome. Were the changes simply formal adaptations of the style of Ancient authors to make it more palatable?

Montaigne, whose *Essais* were enjoyed by some of the eighteenth-century aristocratic women who hosted the salons of Paris (like the Marquise du Deffand) had, in turn, drawn inspiration from classical authors, and promoted their ideas, while criticizing their style. He claimed, for instance, that reading Cicero was *ennuyeux* because his style was too prolix (1588, fol. 172 r-v, 1613, p. 229, 1685, p. 139) and that Seneca's style was *ennuyeux* because it was repetitious. His remark that repetition is *ennuyeuse* was translated into English by Florio in the early seventeenth century as 'repetition is ever tedious' and by Cotton eighty years later as 'repetition is every where troublesome' (1613, p. 542, 1685, p. 299). This indicates that the complex concept denoted by the French term *ennuyeux* existed among speakers of English before the word 'boring' was introduced.

Prior to the late eighteenth century, the 'sentiments' which writers described or discussed were not the expression of some 'interiority', which we have learned to locate inside the individual's mind (head and/or heart), inspired by the writings of the Romantics and psychoanalysts. It was the Romantic and post-Romantic authors who expected to be able to read about human experience, and who often had little patience with the writings that failed to capture it. Thus, for instance, Flaubert noted in his diary in January 1860: 'virtuous books are so boring [*ennuyeux*] and so false, they fail to recognize human nature and the eternal background of unbridled individual human life, the self against everybody else, individuals against society or outside it, the true organic human being' (Flaubert, 1988, p. 214). Yet the search for authenticity that characterized much of the literature of the nineteenth century was indebted to previous endeavours, and often situated in transcultural contexts.

Earlier I suggested the need for psychologists to take on board recent approaches to the emotions as socially, culturally and historically situated, and to think more about the ways in which emotion is shaped by language. Here I focus on historical emotions, beginning with a discussion of the methods we might use and the perspectives we might take in trying to understand them. The method I choose is necessarily situated, drawing as it does on the hermeneutic practices of those of my predecessors who have tried to understand, and interpret for others, texts written in historical contexts (and sometimes languages) different from their own. But I also seek to draw attention to the interaction between text and image.

2.1 Methodology

One of the most lucid expositions about the situated nature of understanding can be found in Hans-Georg Gadamer's *Wahrheit und Methode* (Truth and Method, 1960). There Gadamer argues that we cannot deny the power of tradition, and that prejudice/prejudgement (*Vorurteil*) has an important role in guiding our choice of (and opening us up to) what is to be understood: 'the recognition that all understanding inevitably involves some prejudice gives the hermeneutical problem its real thrust' (2004, p. 272). He also emphasizes that consciousness is shaped by history, using the phrase *wirkungsgeschichtliches Bewußtsein,* which has been translated as 'historically effected consciousness' (2004, p. 341). He further suggests that understanding creates a new context of meaning, enabling integration of what is otherwise strange, anomalous or unfamiliar (a 'fusion of horizons', *Horizontverschmelzung*) (Vessey, 2009; Malpas and Zabala, 2010; Baum, 2020). More importantly, seeing language as the very medium with which we engage with the world, rather than simply a tool, he stresses that language (and the conceptuality it allows) has a crucial role in hermeneutic experience (Lafont, 1999; Roy and Oludaja, 2009).

The 'experience' to which Gadamer refers is that evoked by the German term *Erfahrung,* from *erfahren,* to gain knowledge. In contrast to lived experience (*Erlebnis*) and to scholarly knowledge (*Wissenschaft*), *Erfahrung* denotes something that happens to us, contrary to our expectations: 'the birth of experience as an event over which no one has control and which is not even determined by the particular weight of this or that observation, but in which everything is co-ordinated in a way that is ultimately incomprehensible' (Gadamer, 2004, p. 347). *Erfahrung* 'is initially always experience of negation: something that is not what we supposed it to be' (2004, p. 349). This is how I invite you to 'experience' the visual and textual material I discuss in this section: letting it surprise you, and make you wonder.

Gadamer distinguishes three approaches to understanding (or experiencing) the other, which are relevant to the study of emotions and states of mind such as boredom. The first approach is that in which researchers maintain a safe distance from their own historicity in the attempt to gain a 'neutral' perspective, and seek to objectify the other by identifying behavioural patterns as a way of predicting future actions. In the second approach, 'one claims to know the other's claim from his point of view and even to understand the other better than the other understands himself' (Gadamer, 2004, p. 353). In the third and 'highest' form of interpersonal and hermeneutic experience, there is mutual understanding, or at least one is open to the other, and this openness involves accepting beliefs and values that may not be in agreement with one's own. As Gadamer puts it: 'openness to the other, then, involves recognizing that I myself must accept some things that are against me, even though no one else forces me to do so' (2004, p. 355). This, in his view, is the essence of 'conversation', in which 'each person opens himself to the other, truly accepts his point of view as valid and transposes himself into the other to such an extent that he understands not the particular individual but what he says' (p. 387).

This is not banal conversation of the kind that produces tedium, discussed or represented in the textual and visual material I present here, but one which involves an open exchange of views and opinions: 'reaching an understanding in conversation presupposes that both partners are ready for it and are trying to recognize the full value of what is alien and opposed to them' (p. 388). As Gadamer further notes, this is the position in which translators find themselves, needing to understand what has been written by another person, as opposed to understanding the author of the text as an individual: 'similarly, the translator must preserve the character of his own language, the language into which he is translating, while still recognizing the value of the alien, even antagonistic character of the text and its expression' (pp. 388–9).

How can we conduct cross-cultural historical research that allows the voices of historical subjects to be heard, in terms which 'we' (researchers and the wider community of readers) can understand? Rather than attempting to adopt a neutral perspective, or to assume that we can impose on cultures from the past the conceptual frameworks and keywords used to explain boredom today, I begin by listening to the terms used in different historical contexts to describe experiences akin to short- and medium-term boredom. I look for evidence of how concepts and terms like *ennui* were translated from one culture to another in early modern bilingual dictionaries, and examine a wide range of early modern translations, in which these terms were used in relation to particular situations and contexts. I also extend Gadamer's approach by considering the beliefs and values transmitted and questioned through visual–textual media like satirical prints, comics and cartoons.

2.2 Terms and Conditions, 1100–1755

Is there much point in studying the history of boredom by looking at the various uses of single keywords? At times psychologists offer impressionistic accounts of the history of boredom by mentioning, for instance, that the French term *ennui* 'was used liberally from the twelfth century onwards, and even infiltrated England towards the end of the seventeenth century' (Martin, Sadlo and Stew, 2006, p. 195; their source is Spacks, 1995). But they fail to take into consideration that, in the twelfth-century *Eneas, enui* denoted profound sorrow (Kuhn, 1976, p. 5) and that the twelfth- and thirteenth-century Provençal troubadors used the term *enuegs* to refer to feelings of vexation and irritation, as well as to the things that provoked those feelings. These are the types of feelings denoted in modern English by the term 'annoy', which has the same etymology as the French *ennui,* the Italian *noia,* and the Spanish *enojo.* Scholars have noted that the French *ennuyer* comes from the Latin *in-odiare,* 'to hold in hatred' (Healy, 1984, p. 18). But no account is taken of the fact that the feelings evoked by *ennuyer* in French and 'to annoy' and 'to weary' in early modern English were often caused by social interactions involving language. An example is the explanation given for the Latin *pertesus* in Elyot's dictionary: 'displeased, annoyed. *Sermonis pertesus,* werye of the communication' (1538, s.v. 'pertesus').

A more significant example of social interaction as a source of *ennui* is found in a hand-written annotation by Montaigne to the 1588 edition of his *Essais,* which refers to the person who seeks solitude as 'celuy qui se retire ennuié et dégousté de la vie commune' (1965, p. 245). In 1603, John Florio rendered this passage into English as 'he that with-drawes himselfe, as distasted and over-tired with the common life', and in the late seventeenth century Charles Cotton translated it as 'he who Retires, weary of, and disgusted, with the common way of Living' (Montaigne, 1613, p. 123, 1685, p. 443). Such notions of psychological tiredness or weariness are associated with boredom to this day, though the English term 'disgust' (unlike the French *dégoût* and the Spanish *asco*) no longer has this meaning. It is only in common parlance that the English phrases 'I am bored of this!', 'I am sick of this!' and 'I am tired of this!' are interchangeable; they are often heard as expressions of the desire (or demand) for a change (e.g., in other people's attitude or behaviour). Curiously, younger people now simply tend to use the word 'bored' (and 'boring'), rather than the alternatives, and say 'I am bored' to demand entertainment and excitement (rather than changes of attitude in others).

Martina Kessel has noted in passing that the concept of ennui as a human condition dates back to the Renaissance and seventeenth-century philosophy of mind (2001, p. 22). However, if we look at autobiographies, historical accounts, fictional writings and bilingual and monolingual dictionaries from the Renaissance, we will also be able to see how the French term *ennui* (like the English 'weariness', the German *Verdruss* and the Spanish *enojo*) denoted not only the sense of satiation or emptiness associated with ennui as a human condition, but a wider range of (potentially transient) interrelated feelings, including chagrin, displeasure, vexation, anger, grief, dismay, unease and annoyance.

The term *ennui* has historically evoked not only boredom, but also heavy feelings like sadness and worry. This is evident, for instance, from the translation of *comblé d'ennui* as 'heaped or filled with heauinesse' in Lucas Harrison's dictionary (Harrison, 1571). That the range of meanings of *ennui* was wide can be seen from the fact that the adjective *ennuyeux* was translated as 'tedyouse or irkesome' (Palsgrave, 1530) and the verb *ennuyer* as 'to molest, to trouble, to weary one' (Harrison, 1571) and 'to annoy; vex, trouble, disquiet, molest; discontent, grieue, afflict, offend; wearie, loath, irke, distast; importune ouermuch' (Cotgrave, 1611). Similarly, the reflexive form *s'ennuyer* was rendered as 'too bee weary of a thing' (Harrison, 1571).

The terms *aburrir* and *aburrido* (which today are usually translated as 'to bore' and 'bored') were used in Early Modern Spain and Spanish America to refer to the extreme state of mind of 'those who are discontented with themselves, heavily disappointed and determined to put an end to it all without thinking of the damage this might cause' (Covarrubias Orozco, 1611, s.v. 'aborrecer'). These terms derived from the Latin *abhorreo,* as did the more educated *aborrecer,* which was defined as: 'to feel aversion towards something, either with fear and horror, or with weariness [*fastidio*]' (1611, s.v. 'aborrecer').

By contrast, the early modern Spanish *enojo* (like the related verb and adjective) had a wider meaning. It was one of the translations for the Latin *taedium* given in Palencia's Latin–Spanish dictionary, alongside 'ansia', 'cuyta', 'aflición' and 'fastidio' (Palencia, 1490, s.v. 'tedium'). Prior to the eighteenth century, *enojo* meant 'heaviness of heart' (*pesadumbre*), 'anger' (*cólera*) or anything that gave one grief, displeasure or concern (*lo que nos da pena y sinsabor*), even though the verb *enojar* was primarily used with the meanings 'to make angry' (*ensañar, poner en cólera*), 'to annoy' or 'to irritate' (*irritar*) (Covarrubias Orozco, 1611, fol. 238v, s.v. 'enojar'). The noun *enojo* later came to denote annoyance or anger (Sobrino, 1734, p. s.v. 'enojo'), but was still used as a translation of the French *ennui* in the early twentieth century (e.g., Payot, 1901, p. 183).

The Latin term *taedium* (which denoted interrelated experiences of 'weariness', 'irksomeness', 'tediousness', 'loathing' and 'disgust') was rendered in English as 'werynes, or heuynes of mynde' (Elyot, 1538, s.v. 'taedium'). 'Tedious', in turn, was one of the English translations for *odiosus,* when referred to a person: 'he that is hated, displesant, troublous, tediouse' (Elyot, 1538, s.v. 'odiosus').

The English 'tediousnes', the Spanish *enojo* and the French *fascherie* were the early modern translations for the Latin word *odium,* used by the humanist Juan Luis Vives (1493–1540) in his influential treatise on the education of women (1523) to describe what mothers would tend to feel while their children were young (1529a, fol. 11r, 1529b, fol. 130r 1579, p. 315, 2002, p. 142). Vives was the first of the sixteenth-century humanists to write on the education of girls and women. Born in Spain, he was based in the Low Countries for most of his adult life, and spent a few years in England in the early 1520s, teaching at Corpus Christi in Oxford and employed at the court of Henry VIII as tutor to his daughter Mary (the future Queen Mary I). His book for women, which he dedicated to Henry's Spanish wife, Catherine of Aragon (Mary's mother), was reprinted time and again in a number of European languages (the English version, by Richard Hyrde, appeared at least eight times in the sixteenth century, in 1529, 1531, 1541, 1547, 1557, 1567, 1585 and 1592).

Rather than trying to assess the extent to which Vives's advice might have been followed by the well-to-do women who read it in their own language in early modern Europe, we can use the translations to gain some insight into the emotional repertoires available to them. But to understand Vives's suggestion about the *odium* ('tediousness', *enojo* or *fascherie*) that might have been felt by the mothers of young children we need to bear in mind that this was a time when infant mortality rates were high (e.g., 15.5 per cent in London in 1539–1599 (Razzell and Spence, 2007, p. 277)). A prominent example is Queen Catherine's only son (Henry VIII's only potential male heir), who lived no more than fifty-three days. How did 'tediousness' feel for women whose main function in life was to produce children, who might not survive? And how did it feel for Queen Catherine to be put aside at the age of forty and banished from the court at forty-eight by a disappointed king still in search of a male heir? The whole range of feelings evoked by the early modern term 'tediousness' come to mind: chagrin, displeasure, vexation, anger, grief, dismay, unease and annoyance.

Nicot's *Thresor de la langue françoyse* (1606) gave both *ennui* and *fascherie* as the translation of a wide range of Latin terms: *aegrimonia*, *aegritudo*, *diuidia*, *incommoditas*, *molestia*, *odium*, *satietas*, *senium*, *taedium* and *fastidium*.[4] The following century, the *Dictionnaire de l'Académie* defined *ennui* as a state of mind caused not only by unpleasant things or events, but also by pleasant things when they went on and on, or when one was not in the right mood for them (3rd ed., 1740, p. 589, s.v. 'ennui'). By the mid-eighteenth century, the French term *ennui* also came to denote the absence of pleasure, rather than chagrin or sadness. As the entry 'Ennui' in the *Encyclopédie ou dictionnaire raisonné des sciences, des arts et des métiers* noted: 'a sort of displeasure difficult to define: it is not chagrin or sadness, but rather the complete lack of pleasure, caused by a *je ne sais quoi* in our organs or in external objects, which, instead of engaging our soul/mind [*âme*], produce an unease or disgust [*dégoût*] to which one cannot get used' (Jaucourt, 1755, p. 693). This development, however, did not make the older meanings of *ennui* obsolete. *Ennui* continued to denote feelings of anguish and sorrow, which can still be evoked by that term today, but are not part of the baggage of the word 'boredom' (Rosen, 2012, p. 349).

Johnson's dictionary, first published in 1755 and reprinted regularly since then, gives a number of examples which show the wide-ranging usage of the term 'tedious' in earlier centuries. It was seen as an equivalent of 'slow' (Johnson, 1755, p. 1180). It evoked feelings like anxiety and impatience related to the slow passage of time, as in Richard Bentley's *Sermons:* 'Sons of the First Men must have a tedious time of Childhood and Adolescence, before they can either themselves assist their Parents, or encourage them with new hopes of Posterity' (Bentley, 1692, pp. 200–1; Johnson, 1755, p. 85). It also described a particular style of writing or talking, as can be seen from Johnson's inclusion of the term 'tedious', alongside 'circumlotory' and 'perplexed, in the list of synonyms of 'ambagious' (1755, p. 119).

For centuries, the English term 'tedious' carried much of the meaning conveyed today by the term 'boring', while other words, like 'tired', were often employed to refer to the state of mind we now call 'boredom'. This latter term was used, for instance, in the 1736 translation of Montesquieu's *Persian Letters* (*Lettres persanes,* 1721) to denote the state of mind which makes Zéphis's slave come up with a few inventions: 'because he was tir'd

---

[4] On the seventeenth-century usage of the term *ennui,* see Dumonceaux (1975), pp. 180–284.

with stayng behind a Door, where I had posted him, he presum'd to suppose he heard or saw what I never did so much as imagine' (Montesquieu, 1736, p. 12). Even though the English 'tir'd' is not as precise as the original French (*il s'ennuie*), the textual context and the situation described makes its meaning clear: Zéphis was fed up with waiting (or bored of waiting), and wished for something to happen.

2.3 Crossing the English Channel: Boring Pleasures and Amusements, 1520–1860

Among the scholars who have portrayed boredom in a positive light in recent years, the philosopher Andreas Elpidorou has suggested that 'the personality trait of boredom can be due to motivational difficulties (when one systematic-ally fails to initiate change), or to cognitive or affective difficulties (when one systematically chooses to alleviate boredom in ways that are ultimately unsat-isfactory), or even to a combination of both' (2018a, p. 475). The idea of boredom as a personality trait dates back to the late 1970s, though the notion that long-term *ennui* could be produced by the failure to satisfy desire (as well as by the satisfaction of all desires) had been discussed in French psychiatry at least four decades earlier (Benon, 1939). Such ideas, however, can be best understood as part of a long history of warnings and regrets related to the obsessive search for pleasure. Even the above definition of the *Dictionnaire de l'Académie* pointed out that repeated or prolonged exposure to pleasant things could produce *ennui*.

Among the early modern moral philosophers who were vociferous in their warnings against idleness, Vives argued that well-to-do mothers who prevented their children from doing any work and making any effort, out of fear that they might become ill (and die), were actually spoiling them and making them weak. His advice was that boys and girls should be taught to read and be kept busy from the age of four or five (as Chryssipus and Quintilian recommend), or the age of seven (as suggested by Aristotle). He also warned that if a girl got tired of reading ('wery of redynge', in Hyrde's translation of 1529; 'lasse de lire', in Pierre de Changy's French translation of 1545), she should not be allowed to be idle. As we can read in a later French translation, which Antoine Tiron dedicated to the two men who had set up a school for girls in the thriving commercial city of Antwerp: 'je ne puis la voir oyseuse' (Vives, 1579, p. 24).

Vives supported his warning against letting girls be idle by referring to the Persian women who spent their lives singing and banqueting in the company of eunuchs, going from one pleasure to another: 'whiche pleasures were ofte chaunged and renewed to eschewe tediousnes: and thende of one pleasure was the begynnynge of another folowynge' (1529a, fol. C4r). 'Tediousness' conveys here the meaning of the Latin *fastidium,* which Vives's modern trans- lator renders as 'boredom' (2000, p. 59); the Latin term, however, expressed a range of sensations and feelings (wider than are usually evoked by the term 'boredom'), from nausea to dislike, disgust and aversion, associated with the satiety produced by excessive pleasure. In the revised Latin version of 1538, Vives expanded this passage, adding that the Persian women found no 'solace' in any of their sensual pleasures, that 'the first savouring of pleasure immedi- ately brought weariness and boredom', and that these women would 'turn away in disgust and incredible anguish from the things they thought would give them most pleasure' (2000, p. 59).

The sense of 'disgust' which Vives described in the first part of the sixteenth century had less to do with physical disgust than with the feeling of weariness (or *lassitude*) identified by writers and artists well into the early twentieth century. It is the satiety which fails to satisfy, which would be captured, for instance, in Adolf Horwicz's *Psychologische Analysen* (Psychological Analyses): 'the sweetest sweets can eventually become completely boring [*langweilig*]' (1875, p. 392). Toohey similarly refers to the 'disgust' caused by repetition: 'when an experience is repeated and repeated and repeated until the person under-going it is utterly 'fed up', they will exclaim that they are bored. Too much baklava can produce this sort of effect. There is usually a flavour of distaste or, more precisely, of disgust that comes about when one is satiated with a situation' (2011, pp. 4–5). But this form of disgust cannot be simply explained as the consequence of repetition. A better explanation is that sensory pleasures (like Horwicz's sweetest sweets and Toohey's baklava) can produce a sense of satiation without ever giving the feeling of satisfaction.

We can discern this form of disgust in seventeen-year-old Flaubert's letter to his friend Ernest Chevalier in 1839:

> I am one of those people who are always disgusted/weary [*dégoûtés*] the following morning, who are always thinking of the future, who are always dreaming, or rather daydreaming, belligerent and plague-stricken, not know- ing what they want, bored [*ennuyés*] of themselves and annoying [*ennuy- ants*]. I went to a brothel to have fun and I got bored .... My existence, which I had dreamed as so beautiful, so poetic, so wide, so romantic, will be like other people's, monotonous, sensible, stupid. (2001, pp. 39–40)

A brothel that might offer sensory pleasure, but not the opportunity to engage one's heart and mind, can satiate rather than satisfy.

Over the centuries, intellectuals, artists and poets alike have often disagreed with the general population about what is entertaining and what is boring. For instance, the philosopher Søren Kierkegaard argued in 1843 that 'idleness as such is by no means a root of evil; on the contrary, it is a truly divine life, if one is not bored' (Kierkegaard, 1987, pp. 289–90). The painter Eugène Delacroix remarked in a diary entry of 11 September 1852 that he had learned from experience that 'too much freedom leads to boredom [*ennui*]' and that solitude was as necessary as distraction (1893, p. 116). In one of the notes jotted by Baudelaire, published posthumously in 1887 as *Mon Coeur mis à nu*, he suggested that 'one must work, if not for pleasure, at least out of despair because, if you think about it, working is less boring than having fun' (2001, pp. x–xi). Baudelaire's suggestion makes sense for those who enjoy their work, as well as for those who, like him, see writing as a necessity, a way of engaging the mind and distracting it from longer-term *ennui,* anxiety and despair.

I mentioned earlier that playful talk about illicit desires and fantasies about transgressive sex have never been restricted to the literate upper classes. Nor has transgressive sex. Nonetheless, it has been the privilege of the powerful and wealthy to indulge in transgressive sex with impunity. For instance, as Edmond Barbier noted in his historical journal of the French court, in 1751, Louis XV's courtiers made every effort to find the king a new mistress because they believed that he needed to be distracted from his fear of the devil, so that he could engage in public life: 'melancholic as he is, he needs entertainment' (1851, p. 232). But, for the next thirteen years, he remained under the influence of Mme de Pompadour, who offered him the variety he so much craved by wearing different dresses every day, filling her room with new curiosities, producing plays in which she always played the starring roles, finding girls to satisfy his sexual appetite and proposing building projects for his pleasure. Her presence at court was deemed essential, as Barbier pointed out in his journal in 1756: 'one must admit that that woman, by her talents and liveliness of character, is, so to speak, necessary to the king, melancholic as he is by nature, who gets bored everywhere' (1856, p. 116; the translation is from Kaiser, 1996, p. 1035). In contrast to today's conceptualization of 'boredom proneness' as a 'personality trait' (e.g., Boden, 2009; questioned in Mercer-Lynn, Bar and Eastwood, 2014), proneness or disposition was then understood in terms of four temperaments; 'melancholy' denoted not only a temperament, but also a disease or condition (marked by unfounded fear and/or sadness), which could be managed through lifestyle changes, such as being 'cheered up'. Being bored was not only the effect of proneness, but also the result of unsatisfying social interactions.

Diderot, one of the best-known non-aristocratic *encyclopédistes,* did much to escape boredom and to expose the transgressive 'sexual playfulness' of the French court in his relatively little-known political satire, *Les Bijoux indiscrets* (1748). This libertine rococo novel aimed to lay bare what was usually 'painstakingly concealed by ignorance, hypocrisy, and falsehood' (Starobinski, 1973, p. 18). The novel was banned, on the basis of its obscenity and its satirizing of court life, and copies of it were confiscated by the police. But the source from which Diderot drew inspiration, the medieval fabliau *Le Chevalier qui fit les cons parler,* continued to circulate, inserted in the Count of Caylus's novel *Nocrion* (1747), in which the fabliau has the overt function of amusing a bored king.

Diderot's novel was not reprinted in French until 1771. In the meantime it circulated in English, in a version published by a clandestine press in London, with the word *bijoux* (a euphemism for genitals) translated as 'toys' (Diderot, 1749). The term *ennui,* which denotes one of the main themes of the novel, was translated into English as 'tiresomeness'.

This example illustrates the fact that in the so-called 'Age of Reason', the very people who promoted rational discourse and logical categorization were also able to indulge in playful satire. Playfulness takes many shapes, and the playfulness with which some of the women at the court of Louis XV sought to counteract their *ennui* or that of their lovers was only one aspect of their lived experience. When it came to chasing away boredom, satire and satirical drawings were equally (if not more) effective. Satire was not only a political tool (Phiddian, 2020); it also offered the (perhaps more satisfying) pleasure of looking at things differently and laughing about situations which might have been difficult to accept or endure. It provided a way of provoking others to think and feel differently.

While some Londoners were enjoying Diderot's satirical novel in English, Samuel Johnson was writing opinion essays, in which he criticized the lifestyle of the wealthy idle with remarks such as 'I eat not because I am hungry, but because I am idle' (27 October 1753). He pointed out that they would be happier if they were industrious. This latter idea was the very title of his essay, 'The pleasures and advantages of industry' (27 November 1753), in which he argued that the lives of the rich and idle were not enviable. As he pointed out, 'many squander their exuberance of fortune in luxury and debauchery', while others

> chase pleasure through all the places of publick resort, fly from London to Bath, and from Bath to London, without any other reason for changing place, … always endeavouring to raise some new desire, that they may have something to pursue, to rekindle some hope which they know will be disappointed, changing one amusement for another which a few months will make equally insipid. (1854, p. 550)

By contrast, those who engaged their minds in the 'acquisition or improvement' of their fortunes, not only 'escape the insipidity of indifference, and the tediousness of inactivity, but gain enjoyments wholly unknown to those, who live lazily on the toil of others' (1854, p. 550). As Johnson suggested, rising to a challenge would produce a sense of hope, a pleasurable feeling, which seemed more important than the joy of achievement. The pleasure of entrepreneurship was felt, whereas, as he claimed in *The Idler* on 18 August 1758, the pleasures which 'the greater part of mankind' publicized were 'counterfeit' (Johnson, 1834, p. 373). He also pointed out, on 26 May 1759, that 'it is necessary to hope, though hope should always be deluded; for hope itself is happiness, and its frustrations, however frequent, are less dreadful than its extinction', while 'pleasure is very seldom found where it is sought' (1834, p. 412).

On 27 October 1759, Johnson wrote about the wealthy idle who would spend the summer in the country because that was the fashion, but would do nothing there other than 'languish some months without emotion or desire', wander in the garden 'without sense of its fragrance', and lie down on a couch 'day after day', 'unwilling to wake, and unable to sleep', whereas in London they would have been busy deciding which clothes to be seen wearing and fantasizing about going to the silk shops. Johnson noted that at this time of the year, as they prepared to return to 'the crowds and noise of the great city', their source of motivation was primarily disgust (weariness or boredom)*:* '[they] know that their desire to return is little more than the restlessness of a vacant mind, that they are not so much led by hope as driven by disgust, and wish rather to leave the country than to see the town' (1834, p. 412). The life which the wealthy idle led in the English countryside in the summer months of the eighteenth century, according to Johnson, sounds boring. But the boredom described by Johnson as lack of 'emotion or desire' (when they knew they had nothing to do, nowhere to go) contrasts with the 'vacant' restlessness they felt as 'disgust', when they had had enough and were ready to move on. It is hardly surprising that in the earliest French version of this essay, published in the volume *Le Paresseux,* in Revolutionary Paris, the phrase 'the restlessness of a vacant mind' was translated as 'le désir de dissiper l'ennui qui les dévore' (1790, p. 136). Restlessness, in other words, has long been recognized as a component of *ennui*.

As regards the word 'bore', when it was first used in the late eighteenth century, it did not refer to a new concept (contrary to what Spacks and other researchers inspired by her have claimed). In the satirical etching in Figure 5, published on 6 April 1782, a 'bore' is sitting at a table with two other men, looking intently at the man on his left, holding the button of his coat and boring him with his reporting of what he is reading in the *Extraordinary Gazette,* while the man on his right falls asleep. The etching shows how, at a time when satire and satirical drawings were becoming increasingly popular, the term 'bore'

Figure 5 A Bore, 1782. © The Trustees of the British Museum

served as a shorthand term to denote those whose tedious conversation was experienced as soporific by some and as annoying by others.

Among those who satirized the social lives of well-to-do Londoners in the late eighteenth century was the merchant John Nixon (1750–1818), whose entry into the city's fashionable circles was facilitated by the wealth he acquired in the Irish trade. One of his etchings (Figure 6) shows the practice of entertaining guests by reading out to them in one of the small private soirées of Georgian London. None of the guests pays attention to the reading: some are busy flirting, while others show their boredom by yawning.

In France, English satirical prints became very popular in the aftermath of the French Revolution. During the Directory and Consulate (November 1795–May 1804), a new type of French social satire, *caricature de moeurs* (focused on social stereotypes, fashion, leisure activities and everyday life), began to appear in print series like Aaron Martinet's *Le Suprême Bon Ton* (Fashion Supreme) and *Le Goût du Jour* (Today's Style), and Pierre La Mésangère's *Le Bon Genre* (The Right Style, the source for Figures 7–9). The print from 1801 (Figure 7) underscores the futility of the lives of those who pursued pleasure in fashionable places like ice cream parlours: it shows three ladies eating ice cream at a table, one of whom seems unsatisfied, ready to order again from the list of flavours displayed by the waiter, while the other two look unengaged, or bored perhaps. That such ladies were 'bored' was suggested by the title of the print Les Ennuyées de Longchamp, published in 1805 (Figure 8). The ways in which the

Figure 6 John Nixon, Interior with a fat woman reading aloud, 1788.
© The Trustees of the British Museum

Figure 7 Les Glaces (The Ice Creams), 1801. © The Trustees of the British
Museum

Figure 8 Les Ennuyées de Longchamp, 1805. © The Trustees of the British Museum

well-to-do sought to entertain themselves were also parodied in the print 'Les Chiens à la Mode (Fashionable Dogs)', from 1808, which shows dogs, dressed as humans, being made to dance under their instructor's whip (Figure 9).

Before the Revolution, Longchamp had been visited by the aristocracy for the religious concerts held at the Abbey on three Easter days each year. Now, in the early nineteenth century, it was the place where the wealthy idle and those who wanted to appear wealthy took fashionable *promedades* (walks), supposedly as exercise, following hygienic advice. But they were less concerned with their health than with appearances. As an article in the *Gastronome* suggested in 1830, some people went without food to be able to buy and display fashionable outfits and hats. Their walks at Longchamp were opportunities to fantasize about impressing others with their looks: 'How many bored people, blasé little mistresses, busy husbands, idle young men, dream, a fortnight before, of the impression they will make and, a fortnight later, of the impression they have made' (Lacroix, 1830, p. 4).

Satirical prints travelled fast across geographical and linguistic borders. This can be seen, for instance, in Figure 10, a copy in reverse, attributed to Thomas Rowlandson, of Pierre Nolasque Bergeret's *Les Musards de la Rue du Coq* (The

Figure 9 Les Chiens à la Mode (Fashionable Dogs), 1808. CCØ
Paris Musées / Musée Carnavalet – Histoire de Paris

Figure 10 Thomas Rowlandson (after Pierre Nolasque Bergeret), *Les Musards de la Rue du Coq* (Dawdlers of the Rue du Coq), ca. 1805–1819. © The Trustees of the British Museum

Dawdlers of the Rue du Coq, 1803). It shows a crowd competing to look at caricatures in the windows of Aaron Martinet's print-shop, at 124 rue du Coq Saint Honoré, in Paris. This copy, printed by Thomas Tegg in London between 1805 and 1819, cleverly adds to the scene an advert for the caricatures published by Tegg. Bergeret's *Les Musards* was also published in Germany in 1806.

In late eighteenth- and early nineteenth-century England, the affluent thought they were embracing modernity by trying to catch up with the latest fashion in clothing and being seen in fashionable places like Bath and Cheltenham; an example of this was the son of King George III, a target of the caricaturists of his day. Upward social mobility was an important goal not only for the urban classes, but also for small landowners and farmers who benefited from the scarcity and inflation created by Britain's wars with France, and now had the means to educate their children in boarding schools. The social aspirations of newly prosperous farmers were decried in publications such as the *Gentleman's Magazine* (A Southern Faunist, 1801, p. 588) and in satirical prints, like 'Farmer Giles & His Wife' (Figure 11). Published in 1809, this etching shows sixteen-year-old Betty, who has been able to avoid the old world of her parents' farm by being sent to boarding school, and is now back home, entertaining proud family members with her piano playing and singing, and her accomplishments in

Figure 11 James Gillray (after Lt-Col Thomas Braddyll), Farmer Giles and his wife shewing off their daughter Betty to their neighbours, on her return from school, 1809. © The Trustees of the British Museum

drawing and embroidery. The fashionable high-waisted gowns and simple hairstyles of the new generation (Betty and another girl) contrast with the dated clothes and hairstyles of the neighbours, who wear low-wasted gowns and fichus, and particularly with the old-fashioned powdered wig worn by the seated neighbour, who is looking utterly bored. This man's bored expression suggests not only that modernity meant different things to different people, but also that boredom was not a product of modernity.

In the early nineteenth century, as before, boredom continued to be the result of unsatisfying social interactions. As historical trends and changes in fashion redirected people's goals and aspirations, the intersubjective, interpersonal dimension of boredom was less subject to change. The moderns and early moderns were probably as bored by the displays of musical ability of other people's children as most of us, post-moderns, might be if made to watch other people's children's school shows.

Alasdair MacIntyre suggests that those for whom the social world is nothing but a 'meeting place of individual wills' and 'an arena for the achievement of their own satisfaction' will no doubt realize that the 'last enemy is boredom' (1981, p. 25). In the early nineteenth century, when an increasing number of leisure activities were organized in grand venues like theatres and opera houses, wealthy people flocked to them wanting to be entertained, and to be seen. Some of these shows were run for large numbers of people who paid different amounts. But the experience was not necessarily more satisfying for those who paid more. This is suggested in the satirical print in Figure 12, published in Paris in 1818, which depicts a performance of the opera *La morte di Semiramide*, by the Portuguese composer Marcos António da Fonseca, with the internationally acclaimed Italian soprano Angelica Catalani singing the title role and her French husband and manager, Paul de Valabrègue, calling out to her from the wings: 'Wife, wife, do not forget the trill [*Ma femme, ma femme, n'oublie pas la roulade*]'. This hand-coloured satirical drawing seems to be based on an actual performance in London's King's Theatre, Haymarket, on 13 December 1806 (Catalani stayed in London until 1813 and returned there in 1818). The text accompanying it indicates that the members of the audience who occupy free seats are ecstatic with the opera performance, while those in paid seats are bored. Perhaps 'looking bored' was no more than a pose, in response to trills, by those who thought them incompatible with truly refined taste. In any case, the people in the front row in this French caricature from 1818 appear to be experiencing what, sixty years later, in *Human, All too Human* (1878; first published in English in 1908), Nietzsche would name the 'ennui of the most subtle and cultured brains' (Maxim 369; 2012, p. 352). It seems as if the phenomenon existed before it was identified as a sociocultural pattern, before it was given a name.

Figure 12 Anon., Angelica Catalani as Semiramis in the opera 'La morte di Semiramide'. Coloured engraving, 1818. Wellcome Collection

If pleasant experiences could become tedious through repetitiveness, it was often in their aftermath that tediousness or *ennui* would be felt most strongly. This was noted not only by Flaubert, as we saw earlier, but also by a few of his contemporaries on both sides of the Atlantic. As Florencio María del Castillo (1828–1863) pointed out in his novella *Culpa* (Guilt), first published in Mexico in 1854:

> There is nothing more monotonous, nothing more tiring [*cansado*] and tedious [*tedioso*] than the hours that follow a ball; it seems as if the soul and the body are equally exhausted. The harmony of the music is followed by a buzzing in the ears; the pleasure derived from the sense of sight is followed by some sort of dazzle; the smiles of joy are followed by the forced smile of weariness [*hastío*]. (Castillo, 1872, p. 391)

The tediousness and weariness experienced by the well-to-do and their imitators in late eighteenth and early nineteenth-century Europe does not seem to have differed much from that of their counterparts in the Americas. We begin to see how the experience of boredom is culturally bound, but also how culture is not bound by geographical or linguistic barriers.

2.4 Between Monotony and Saturation: Paris, Buenos Aires and Madrid, 1820–1900

In his *Essais de psychologie contemporaine,* first published in 1883, Paul Bourget noted that *ennui* was the modern term for *taedium vitae,* which had always been 'the secret worm of those who have everything they need [*le ver secret des existences comblées*]' (1887, p. 14). But how about the *aburrimiento* of the poor and oppressed? We find an example of this feeling in *El Grito Argentino,* an anti-government newspaper printed by Argentinian émigrés in Montevideo, which had a wide clandestine circulation in Buenos Aires. As the issue of 24 February 1839 suggested, in Argentina there were no longer political factions (Federalists and Unitarists), since all its people were 'fed up (*aburridos*) and despairing at the extent of the crimes, oppression and humiliation' they had had to endure (*El Grito Arjentino,* 1839, p. 1). *Aburridos* evokes here feelings of satiety and dissatisfaction, the extreme state of mind, related to desperation, that this term had denoted in the early seventeenth century.

Similar feelings of dissatisfaction, of being 'fed up', had been depicted in a drawing by Charles Joseph Traviès published in *La Caricature morale, religieuse, littéraire et scénique* (Figure 13) on 27 October 1831, which showed exhaustion, hunger, powerlessness and despair on the faces of unemployed artisans and factory workers. Traviès's drawing was not a caricature, but was as revolutionary as many examples of that genre in that it challenged the image of French workers as heroic and hardworking that had been promoted in the visual arts in the aftermath of the Revolution of July 1830. In France, it was the two big industrialized cities, Paris and Lyon (with 785,862 and 160,000 inhabitants, respectively, according to the 1831 census) that were suffering most acutely the effects of the economic depression which was affecting the whole of Western Europe. The feelings of weariness of the unemployed depicted by Traviès clearly differed from the weariness and disgust associated with sensory excess (discussed by Vives, Horwicz and Toohey). The weariness brought about by unemployment among those who had migrated to the city for work also differed from the sense of having nothing to do which Johnson had identified among the rich idle in the English countryside a century earlier. While the rich idle could try to escape boredom by travelling, the forced inaction of the poor idle, the *désoeuvré,* would have typically led to a sense of weariness, marked by hunger and desperation, and of being stuck, having nowhere to go.

Figure 13 Charles Joseph Traviès, 'Peuple affranchi' (1831), CCØ Paris
Musées / Musée Carnavalet – Histoire de Paris

One of the situations in which forced inactivity produced weariness or
boredom (*ennui*) in the nineteenth century was transatlantic travel, involving
people of diverse social and cultural backgrounds, like the hundreds of British
and Irish migrants who travelled to Buenos Aires in cargo ships loaded with
textiles, hardware and ceramics in the early 1820s, or the several hundred
British passengers (mostly migrants) carried by the forty ships which landed
in Argentina in the second half of 1825 (Rock, 2018, pp. 56, 58). As the French
botanist and explorer Arsène Isabelle pointed out in an account of his voyage to
South America in 1830–1834:

> The life of a passenger is really monotonous, one needs to admit, particularly
> for those who are insensitive to the imposing spectacle of the many marvel-
> lous scenes offered by nature, whose spirit is preoccupied only with his future
> plans. He just has a fixed idea: to arrive early at his destination. Boredom
> [*ennui*], furthermore, is a gnawing worm, produced by leisure, which attacks
> relentlessly those who are unoccupied. (1835, p. 46)

According to Isabelle, boredom was not produced by the idleness imposed by
circumstances, in the confined space of a ship, but by impatience, by wanting to
get somewhere and do something. Nonetheless, in claiming that he avoided
getting bored by contemplating the wonderful views from the ship, Isabelle was

taking for granted a privilege from which migrant travellers would have been excluded. If migrants, who usually travelled in crammed conditions, with reduced access to food, drink, light and sanitary facilities, had felt anything akin to boredom, their experience would probably have had less to do with monotony than with deprivation (eating dull dry food or going hungry) and saturation (e.g., being tired of other people's noises and smells).

Isabelle went on to discuss in passing the role of culture in shaping the experience of boredom. He suggested that a western baby brought up by 'savages' away from his home environment would become accustomed to the sensory impressions made by 'the weather, the land, the food and the environment' and would not envy any of the 'pleasures' of the civilized world when reaching the age of reason; if he then was placed in a big city, he would feel dizzy and would sigh, missing the land in which he was brought up; at a luxurious party, he would certainly 'get bored to death' (*mourra d'ennui*) (1835, pp. 52–3).

As regards city life, Isabelle noted that the atmosphere of Buenos Aires changed three times a day. The vibrancy felt there in the morning and evening would give way to what he perceived as the 'monotony and the silence of death' at *siesta* time (2–5 pm): everyone stopped working because it was too hot, and the streets were completely deserted; all that could be seen were the bodies of newspaper sellers sleeping on the pavements (1835, p. 234). In the evening, the high-society women could be seen at the theatre, wearing on their heads *peinetones* which measured up to 1.10 m in width (1835, p. 191).

The Genevan lithographer César Hipólito Bacle (1794–1838), who spent the last ten years of his life in Buenos Aires, produced a satirical series of litographs, titled *Extravagancias de 1834,* which exaggerated the size of the *peinetones* and their effects on other people in public spaces like a street, promenade or a ball, where they needed to be dodged. At the theatre, they obstructed men's view of the stage or prevented them from sitting down, as shown in the lithograph in Figure 14. There we see a curious contrast between the men who chat to one another, perhaps to alleviate boredom, in the private space created by one of the *peinetones,* and the man who sits alone and seeks to escape boredom (or frustration) by trying to sleep, as the lettering suggests: 'it is impossible to see anything with these screens! –So I might just fall asleep'.

Argentina was one of the two major destinations (alongside Brazil) of the nearly five million Spaniards who migrated to the Americas between 1846 and 1932. Of the seven million migrants who arrived in Argentina in 1870–1930, the majority came from Spain and Italy, with one in three Spaniards and one in four Italians settling in Buenos Aires. During that period, Buenos Aires became one

Figure 14 César Hipólito Bacle, Peinetones en el teatro (*Peinetones* at the theatre). Serie Extravagancias de 1834 N°4. Water-coloured lithograph on paper, 18.5 × 24 cm, Buenos Aires, 1834. Museo de Arte Hispanoamericano 'Isaac Fernández Blanco', Gobierno de la Ciudad de Buenos Aires – Argentina

of the world centres of culture. Its booming illustrated press produced significant political satires, such as those published by the French graphic artist Henri Stein in his magazine *El Mosquito* (1863–1893) and those of the Spanish graphic artist Eduardo Sojo, who arrived in Buenos Aires in 1883 and launched the satirical magazine *Don Quijote* the following year. Sojo used humour, under the pseudonym Demócrito, to defend the interests of ordinary Argentines against the country's corrupt political leadership and inefficient administrative and judicial practices. One of his satirical drawings from the series Plagues of Buenos Aires (Figure 15) shows people turned into skeletons, having queued for the best part of a year, while the judge (according to the notice on the door) is on a tour of Europe. This satirical attack on political corruption offers an example of how the sense of being stuck (that is often part of the experience of boredom) might be inflicted from above.

Figure 15 Demócrito (Eduardo Sojo), 'The plagues of Buenos Aires' (Detail), *Don Quijote*, 30 August 1896, p. 2. The Rare Book & Manuscript Library University of Illinois at Urbana-Champaign

Among the short-lived periodicals intended for a female readership which promoted women's education and emancipation in Argentina, *La Ondina del Plata* (1875–1880) became the venue of a powerful campaign by female writers in favour of women in professional careers. *La Ondina* also included an illustrated fashion section, which promoted consumerism as a cure for boredom. For instance, during the carnival of 1879, it referred to the 'snazzy and elegant dresses' of the young ladies, suggesting that 'variety' is more than a source of pleasure; it is 'one of the greatest laws of the world, since where there is no variety, there is only monotony' and 'monotony is the tomb of good taste, liveliness and pleasantness' (Lelia, 1879, p. 90; cited in Vicens, 2014, pp. 103–4).

The emphasis on variety and novelty of the bourgeois women of Buenos Aires was modelled on the splendour of Paris, which would soon seem to prove nauseating. This, at least, was the message conveyed by Zola's *Nana* (1880), in which the crowds of Paris become weary, disgusted with life, and eventually 'succumb to feelings of dullness and stupor', to the apathy that had come to be seen as the *mal-du-siècle* (Rossi, 2018, p. 286). Zola's protagonist, Nana, ends up feeling the emptiness which results from the constant fulfilment of desires:

> Yet, in the midst of her luxury, in the midst of that court, Nana was bored to death [*s'ennuyait à crever*]. She had men with every minute of the night, and money everywhere, even in the drawers of her dressing-table amongst her combs and brushes; but that no longer satisfied her, she felt a void somewhere, a vacancy that made her yawn. Her life rolled on unoccupied, bringing each day the same monotonous hours. (Zola, 1922, p. 276, 1880, p. 354)

But Nana is not the only character who is bored. The staff of foreign embassies are also described as so *blasé* (translated in 1922 as 'so sick of everything') and so 'empty' (*vide,* translated as 'worn out') that they do not even touch the girls who are paid to entertain them (Zola, 1880, p. 478, 1922, p. 373).

—Mi
es por

—Si yo encontrara una mujer rica
que me sacara de esa maldita oficina...

Figure 16 'If only I found a rich woman who could get me out of this damned office', *La caricatura,* Madrid, 14 May 1893. Biblioteca Nacional, Spain

The ostentatious fashion seen in the streets of big cities like Paris, Buenos Aires, New York, Berlin, Barcelona or Madrid in 1800–1900, and the extravagant outfits depicted in the fashion pages of the illustrated press during the latter part of that century, did not only offer sensory variety to help well-to-do women cope with the monotony of their everyday lives. It also became the object of male fantasies. We find an example of such daydreaming in a cartoon published in Madrid in 1893 (Figure 16), in which a bored-looking office worker fantasizes about meeting a wealthy woman who might enable him to give up his job. For bored people wanting to be (doing or feeling) something else, somewhere else, daydreaming (like other distractions) has offered, and will continue to offer, temporary relief (by turning attention away from the passage of time, and from the self). But daydreaming does not help to combat the feelings of dissatisfaction, frustration and emptiness associated with longer-term boredom.

2.5 New Forms of Boredom in the Twentieth Century?

In his essay 'Die Großstädte und das Geistesleben' (The Metropolis and Mental Life, 1903), the sociologist Georg Simmel echoed the long-standing view that excessive exposure to sensual/sensory pleasures leads to *fastidium,* but explained it in the scientific terms available in his age: 'immoderately sensuous life makes one blasé [*blasiert*] because it stimulates the nerves to their utmost reactivity until they finally can no longer produce any reaction at all' (2002, p. 14; cf. 1995, p. 121). He then drew on this observation to explain, by analogy, that less harmful stimuli can also exhaust the strength of the nerves if they are rapid and contradictory, as they are in big cities. The overstimulating city environment creates nervous exhaustion and thus blunts the ability of urban dwellers to react to new sensations, making them prone to develop a 'blasé attitude'. This, as Simmel suggested, is why this kind of attitude could be identified in children who grew up in large cities, but not in those raised in more peaceful and stable milieus. He further argued that, besides physiological causes, the 'blasé attitude' is also derived from a money economy, which makes people value things only in terms of how much they cost, and become 'indifferent' to those things in themselves, experiencing them as 'meaningless', 'homogeneous', 'flat' and grey' (2002, p. 14; cf. 1995, p. 121).

Simmel also noted that, in contrast with the familiarity and vibrancy with which people from small towns tend to greet one another, the personal encounters in the metropolis are fleeting and thus flat: investing time or emotion on them is not worthwhile. Modern sensibility is driven by a yearning for extreme impressions, a craving for excitement. The thrills offered by popular entertainments, which in Simmel's day also included cinema, were making people addicted to sensations of novelty, to excitement and to the shock experienced when exposed to surprise. The problem was that frequent exposure to excitement was counterproductive, as Simmel put it elsewhere, using an analogy from one of the latest technologies, which seemed rather pertinent:

> With reference to electric shock treatment, it has been observed that frequent repetition may turn the result into its opposite and again into the opposite of the opposite. It is an everyday experience of major and typical importance that almost all pleasure-affording stimuli can, after an original increase in pleasurable sensation, lead to its arrest and even to positive pain. (2004, pp. 263–4)

If, in earlier times, it was too much partying (or too much travelling between London and Bath for no purpose other than to be seen) that was found boring by some, now the mere fact of living in a big city, exposed to an overload of information and sensory impressions, was thought to have a dulling effect on the senses, and to lead to estrangement and apathy.

In some big cities, however, tradition placed limits on people's everyday experience of pleasure-affording stimuli. This is exemplified in the accounts, published in the Catalan satirical magazine *L'Esquella de la Torratxa* in 1913, of the Easter Week activities of Senyor Esteve, the prototype of the wealthy but narrow-minded male shopkeeper from Barcelona (based on a character from Santiago Rusiñol's novel of 1907). Prudenci Bertrana's textual satire of 21 March stresses how, being forced to give up his routines (like travelling by tramway, playing domino in the café, and watching international *vedettes* at the theatre), Senyor Esteve would walk instead with his wife from church to church, 'looking bored' (*aire avorrit*), 'putting on a well-rehearsed gravity which does not come from inside' (1913, p. 195). A series of vignettes published in the same issue of *L'Esquella* show churchgoing as the main practice at Easter, when frivolous entertainment was not available (Figure 17). Expected to listen to long sermons, people would seek to escape boredom by falling asleep (Figure 18), or by looking for alternative sensory stimuli (e.g., Senyor Esteve ogling the woman behind him at church in Figure 19). It may well be that, in restricting people's access to sensory pleasure, religious traditions have produced short-term boredom, while also serving to prevent the long-term apathy and indifference which Simmel associated with modern city life.

In a modern metropolis like Barcelona, with a sizable bourgeois population, restaurants offered a consumerist alternative (i.e., stake) to traditional religious practices of abstinence and restraint, which women were expected to adhere to and promote at home (a situation parodied in Figure 20). This suggests that, when seeking to understand how people might have experienced boredom in the past, we should avoid making simplistic distinctions between urban and rural life.

Figures 17, 18, 19 and 20 Senyor Esteve at Easter, *L'Esquella de la Torratxa*,
21 March 1913. Virtual Library of Historical Newspapers, Spain

Figures 17, 18, 19 and 20 (cont.)

—Què't sembla, Esteve, aquest monument?
—Déu n'hi doret!... De tots els que he vist, és el que més m'agrada.

Figures 17, 18, 19 and 20 (cont.)

—Hi hà sopa de peix...
—No. Porta'm un bon «bistec», que'm tregui el regust del bacallà de casa.

Figures 17, 18, 19 and 20 (cont.)

We should also consider how traditional modes of thinking and living coexisted with so-called modernity, and how coexisting attitudes and practices were shaped by gender and class differences.

Boredom has taken many shapes even within particular socio-historical contexts. For instance, 'boredom' (*avorriment*) might be characterized by frustration and annoyance, particularly when associated with physical pain. We can see this in Rusiñol's letter to his friend Joan Alcocer in October 1913: 'I have been having a hard time, with pain in my feet and legs. Every now and then I have to spend a few days in bed, and this (the inconvenience and the suffering) really makes me bored/annoyed [*avorrit*]. It must be that I'm getting old' (Laplana, 1995, p. 410).

In turn, boredom in the workplace could be interpreted in relation to modern medical categories like 'neurasthenia', rather than to seemingly outdated moral paradigms. Thus, for instance, we can hear Marcel, a decadent Modernist poet In Rusiñol's play *La intel·lectual* (1909), complaining of 'a boredom at work which, if I did not know where it is coming from [i.e., neurasthenia], could be mistaken for laziness [*un avorriment al treball que, si no que ja sé lo que és, qualsevol diria que és mandra*]' (Rusiñol, 1947, p. 144). This is clearly a parody of the increasingly widespread use among well-to-do Spaniards in the early twentieth century of the medical label 'neurasthenia', coined by the physician George Miller Beard in North America in 1869 (to refer to the 'nervous exhaustion' that was becoming prevalent there).

Traditional religious concepts such as 'laziness' coexisted with moral discourses about 'aboulia' (weakness of the will) and with medical categories repeatedly promoted by advertisements in the press of products like Koch's tonic, which promised to cure a range of conditions and feelings in men, including neurasthenia, headache, constipation, tinnitus, memory loss and boredom (*El Liberal*, 1900; *ABC*, 1903; *Nuevo Mundo*, 1909b), or Hoffmann's drops, intended for neurasthenics and those 'bored with life' (*Nuevo Mundo*, 1909a). The magazines in which such adverts were placed would occasionally show awareness of social differences in the experience of boredom, as in Dionisio Pérez's remark that, in the outskirts of Madrid, 'poor people are bored and desperate' (1909).

In the early twentieth century, the media were also making people increasingly aware of the fact that feelings of boredom could be experienced as the result of disappointment, at events anticipated to be exciting, like a carnival ball or a football match. An example of boredom linked to disappointment was reported by the Bilbao sports paper *Los Deportes* at a time when most of Europe was involved in the First World War: 'we expected that the match between the Madrid team and Bilbao's Athletic would be like a cyclone, that we would shout, whistle and clap like madmen/fanatics [*energúmenos*], ... but we got bored rigid [*nos hemos aburrido como ostras*]' (1916, p. 16). This is an example of the expectations created in those who had access to purchased leisure activities: people who paid to be aroused felt frustrated if they were not.

Carnival, in turn, offered the opportunity to indulge in immoderate pleasure and excitement for a short-period, before the restrictions of Lent. But it was experienced in different ways by different people, as can be seen in the following fictional dialogue, from 1916, between a man who sees carnival balls as 'festivals of the joy of living', bursting with happiness (*esclat de l'alegría*), and another who wants to ban them, based on his experience of them as boring, sad events:

> I too have been to Carnival balls, and still go sometimes. And I have seen that there usually is not any of such joy or such delights there. All I have been able to see there is boredom (*avorriment*), tiredness, disgust [*fàstic*], sleepiness [*sòn*], sadness. A sadness hovering with *confetti,* twisted with serpentines, sweetened with sweets, drowned by the sound of music. (*L'Esquella de la Torratxa*, 1916)

—Les monges ens han dit que és pecat. Ai, ai!...
Elles be hi van, de distreçades!...

Figure 21 Back from the Carnaval ball, *L'Esquella de la Torratxa*, 3 March 1916 Virtual Library of Historical Newspapers, Spain

Next to the dialogue is a vignette (Figure 21) depicting a girl returning from a carnival ball. The accompanying text suggests that the nuns who claimed that going to the carnival ball was sinful were there themselves, hiding behind their fancy dresses. Historically, carnival masks have served not only to hide hypocrisy, but also to put on hold people's feelings of boredom and disappointment.

As regards English-speaking contexts, it was in the early twentieth century that terms like 'bored' and 'boredom' began to be used more widely. At that time, these terms tended to convey the effect of monotony, the feelings which Virginia Woolf tried to avoid by turning away from what her society expected of well-to-do women. As she put it in her diary: 'boredom is the legitimate kingdom of the philanthropic. They rule in the metropolis' (1977, vol. I: 192). Her main way of alleviating her own boredom was by writing: 'the great thing is never to feel bored with one's own writing. That is the signal for a change – never mind what, so long as it brings interest' (1977, vol. II: 292). In her diary notes, she not only described how difficult it was to have to talk to servants during the air raids of the First World War because (rather snobbishly) she found them 'dull' (1977, vol. I: 85). She also interpreted the boredom she experienced during the war as her contribution to the war effort, while remaining acutely aware of the effect of social conditioning: 'we pay the penalty for our rung in society by infernal boredom' (1977, vol. V: 288 and 357).

Nonetheless, terms like 'bore' and 'bored' were not only used in the context of monotony, lack of stimulation or sensory deprivation. Even a 'modern' character like Constance Chatterley in D. H. Lawrence's *Lady Chatterley's Lover* (1928) gets bored in different ways, which are clear to the reader from the situation. For instance, when she walks to the game-keeper's house with her daughter, she is 'well bored' by her before they get there; she has had enough of the girl's tricks, and of her being 'so self-assured' (Lawrence, 2002, p. 60). Her boredom in that particular situation is not caused by under-stimulation, but seems rather a state of satiety and annoyance.

The German writer, journalist, sociologist, cultural critic and film theorist Siegfried Kracauer evoked even more intense feelings of saturation in an article published in the *Frankfurter Zeitung* on 16 November 1924, in which he claimed that the cheap and ubiquitous entertainment offered in the western metropolis was to blame for hijacking people's spirits. In 'streets replete with unfulfillment' in the shape of glowing street adverts promising alcohol and cigarettes, people were becoming unable to feel their emptiness (1995, p. 331). Cinemas created the illusion of 'a life that belongs to no one and exhausts everyone' (p. 332). Radio broadcasts were turning people's heads into a 'playground for worldwide noises', letting individuals be 'appropriate[d]' by the 'boundless imperialism' of cultures from the 'five continents' (p. 333). As Kracauer suggested, it was not the easily dispelled 'vulgar boredom of daily drudgery', the dissatisfaction experienced by those 'whose duties occasionally make them yawn' that one should worry about, but the dullness of 'those who do their business by inclination', who were being 'pushed deeper and deeper into the hustle and bustle until eventually they no longer know where their head is' (p. 332). Frivolous forms of entertainment only created 'inner restlessness without a goal, a longing that is pushed aside, and a weariness with that which exists without really being' (p. 334). The remedy which Kracauer proposed for the alienation caused by modernity is the 'extraordinary, radical boredom' of taking a break from all activity, from all the amusements and distractions that surround one, and simply to be (or learn to be) with oneself: 'on a sunny afternoon when everyone is outside, one would do best to hang about in the train station or, better yet, stay at home, draw the curtains, and surrender oneself to one's boredom on the sofa . . . until eventually one becomes content to do nothing other than be with oneself, without knowing what one actually should be doing' (p. 334). This would require one to have 'patience' but, in his view, it was the only way to gain 'control of one's own existence' (p. 334).

The most persuasive part of Kracauer's argument is his opening idea: that those who have leisure time but choose not to be bored are 'certainly just as boring as those who never get around to being bored'; they are boring because 'their self has vanished' (p. 331). His concept of *Langeweile* as a quiet time when nothing happens around oneself was clearly different from his notion of *langweilig,* which described the effect that alienated people had on others. While Kracauer's *radikale Langeweile* can be related to the solitude which, throughout the centuries, has been sought by those who (like Montaigne) found other people boring, his use of the adjective *langweilig* evokes a sense of annoyance and aversion, denoted in other languages by terms like *ennui, noia* and 'boredom'.

In a series of lectures delivered in Freiburg in 1929–1930, the German philosopher Martin Heidegger explained boredom as a relational and ambivalent category, seeking to transcend the then prevalent taxonomy of boredom (*ennui* or *Langeweile*) as lack, loss or absence. He distinguished between three types of boredom: 'becoming bored by something' (*Gelangweiltwerden von etwas*), 'being bored with something' (*das Sichlangweilen bei etwas*) and the deep boredom experienced when one tells oneself 'I am bored' (*es ist einem langweilig*), rather than saying it aloud (1983, p. 163). The first type of boredom, characterized by the sensation that time is stretching before oneself, is caused by events and objects, such as a train delay, which leaves one stuck, waiting in a provincial station, or a book which one continues to read despite finding it boring: 'in becoming bored by something we are precisely still held fast by that which is boring, we do not yet let it go, or we are compelled by it, bound to it for whatever reason, even though we have previously freely given ourselves over to it' (1995, p. 92). In the second type of boredom (experienced, for instance, when thinking about the previous night's perfectly pleasant dinner party), it feels as if time stands still, but this feeling cannot be blamed on any object:

> In being bored with ... a certain detachment from that which is boring has already occurred. That which is boring is indeed at hand, yet we are bored without that which is boring specifically or explicitly boring us; we are bored—almost as though the boredom came from us and as though the boredom continued to propagate itself, without needing to be caused by or bound to what is boring any more. (1995, p. 92)

In the most profound form of boredom, there is complete indifference, other people and the whole world become undifferentiated, unengaging and distant, and one loses one's recognizable traits, 'name, standing, vocation, role, age and fate' (1995, p. 135; Hammer, 2004). As Heidegger pointed out, this third type of boredom is not an emotion, but a fundamental mood (*Grundstimmung*), which enables philosophical inquiry by allowing us to detach ourselves from everyday concerns and to see ourselves for what we really are.

Heidegger's generic types of boredom, identifiable in people of comparable socio-economic status (SES) in his century and ours (those with time to read, opportunities to go to pleasant dinner parties and a penchant for philosophical inquiry), contrast with the more historically bound forms of boredom distinguished by the German-Jewish philosopher and critical theorist Walter Benjamin in works written in Paris in the 1920s and 1930s. Benjamin (like Simmel and Kracauer) warned that the repeated overstimulation and shocks of modern life and labour were responsible for the state of hyper-alertness and unresponsiveness (and the seemingly shallow and disconnected experience) of modern city dwellers (see Salzani, 2009). But he also evoked an idealized, relaxed, semi-unconscious, self-forgetful, receptive state of mind, attributing it to people who engaged in traditional activities, like weaving and spinning, which were slowly disappearing. It was this relaxed state of mind that he had in mind when he complained, in a piece published in the *Frankfurter Zeitung* in November 1932, that there was not enough boredom (*Langeweile*) around for storytelling to continue to flourish: 'people who are not bored cannot tell stories. But boredom no longer has any room in our lives' (1991). In 'The Story Teller', published in 1936, he warned again about the detrimental effects on human experience of the loss of traditional ways of working and socializing:

If sleep is the apogee of physical relaxation, boredom is the apogee of mental relaxation. Boredom is the dream bird that hatches the egg of experience. . . . the activities that are intimately associated with boredom – are already extinct in the cities and are declining in the country as well. With this the gift for listening is lost and the community of listeners disappears. (1968, p. 91).

In the *Arcades Project,* conceived in Paris in 1927 and still in progress when he fled the Occupation, Benjamin referred to *Langeweile* as 'the external surface of unconscious events', and described it metaphorically as 'a warm grey fabric lined on the inside with the most lustrous and colourful of silks', in which 'we wrap ourselves when we dream' (1999, pp. 105–6). He also suggested that *Langeweile* is a fruitful state of mental openness, attainable by allowing oneself to go beyond habitual expectations, and habitual inter-pretations: 'we are bored [*Langeweile haben wir*] when we don't know what we are waiting for. That we do know, or think we know, is nearly always the expression of our superficiality or inattention. Boredom is the threshold of great deeds' (1999, p. 105).

Modern city life did not bring with it a modern form of boredom, as has been often claimed. It brought a greater and more widespread sense of alienation and apathy, which, by the early twentieth century, was accentuated not only by the increasingly prevailing money economy (Simmel) and the proliferation of sources of sensory stimulation (Simmel; Krakauer), but also by the dehumaniz-ing effects of Taylorism (streamlining) in anonymous factory workplaces. The alienation produced by monotonous working practices gave rise to the develop-ment of academic disciplines such as industrial psychology, as we saw earlier. But it also became the target of artistic endeavours such as Charles Chaplin's *Modern Times* (1936), which used visual humour to combat apathy. Cinemas, the main alternative to traditional practices of storytelling, gave large groups of anonymous city dwellers the opportunity to laugh, feel sad and be bored together. It offered people temporary relief from alienating forms of boredom (associated with over-activity, distracted fullness, and tension), while prevent-ing them from feeling emptiness and utter disconnectedness.

Alienation continued to be the focus of artistic and intellectual endeavours, such as Samuel Beckett's 1950s trilogy, which have often been thought of as 'an art of the boring' (Phillips, 2004, p. 252) and as texts designed to 'represent boredom', 'to formally reproduce it', and to induce it in the reader (Pedretti, 2013, pp. 586–7). By the early 1960s, as psychologists (like Berlyne) began to pay attention to states of boredom involving high arousal, the use of the term 'boredom' became increasingly questioned by non-psychologists. For instance, referring to the new art of the 1960s (like Beckett's narratives and Antonioni's films), the philosopher, filmmaker and political activist Susan Sontag claimed that 'there is, in a sense, no such thing as boredom. Boredom is only another name for a certain species of frustration' (1966, p. 303).

Using the categories proposed by the sociologist Martin Doehlemann (1991), scholars now tend to distinguish between the 'situational' and 'existential' forms of boredom (Svendsen, 2005; Toohey, 2011). The former, that which occurs in specific situations, would include Heidegger's first two types of boredom. The latter would overlap with Heidegger's third type. In practice, however, the 'existential'/'situational' distinction often appears blurred, particularly in the everyday language used in the mass media in the last few decades, as we shall now see.

2.6 Boredom and Transience: The Case of Spain, 1975–2000

We find a few examples of the blurred line between 'existential' and 'situational' boredom in the hereto untranslated essays of Eduardo Haro Ibars (1948–1988), one of the pioneers of counterculture during the Spanish Transition. He considered, for instance, the 'pang of boredom and disappointment' felt by children who have too many toys, when they are given the one they had so much wanted and 'they realise they don't like it' (Haro Ibars, 1979a). But he went on to suggest that this had little to do with the kind of boredom available to his generation, who had been deprived of toys, and of a 'real life' (1979a). Following Franco's death in 1975, some of those who had led meaningful lives by opposing Francoism were feeling 'empty', as noted in an editorial of the fringe magazine *Star* (Fernández, 1977).

On the tenth anniversary of André Breton's death, Haro Ibars wrote an article about Dadaism in the magazine *Tiempo de Historia* (1976), in which he quoted the claim made by the Romanian–French avant-garde poet Tristan Tzara (1896–1963) that literature was his antidote against boredom: 'I am not a professional writer and I have no literary ambitions. I should have become a successful adventurer, making subtle gestures, if I had had the physical force and nervous stamina to achieve this one exploit: not to be bored' (Tzara, 1981, p. 87). Haro Ibars would later note that the exiled Spanish poet Luis Cernuda (1902–1963) had abandoned Surrealism in favour of 'new forms of literary combat against the constant tedium of life' (1977, p. 45). Literature, in its constantly changing forms, offers writers and readers transient ways of escaping boredom.

In the wake of the Spanish rural–urban migration since the 1960s, Haro Ibars described non-urban experiences in condescending terms: the 'boring birdsong'; the 'monotony of green fields' in the spring; the '"peace of the countryside", which is the peace of boredom' (1979e). But he also saw the dormitory towns outside Madrid as a 'belt of boredom and hidden poverty [*un cinturón de aburrimiento y miseria vergonzante*]' (1979a). The big city evoked in him two contrary, oscillating feelings: 'the desire to take it over as a creative space' and 'the urge to escape the everyday experience of hell' (Sarría Buil, 2015, p. lxxxii). Some days, as he claimed in an article in *Tiempo de Historia* in March 1979, his state of sadness and of being 'fed-up' (*hastío*) made the doors of the city's cinemas appear to him like 'the mouths of the cold Hell of absolute boredom' (Haro Ibars, 1979g, p. 88). Other times, while at the cinema, he would cease to be bored when the content of the film made him feel indignant; as he noted, 'indignation is a powerful drug that makes one forget one's boredom' (1979g, p. 89).

One of the cultural changes of the Spanish Transition was the restoration in 1977 of the carnival celebrations, outlawed since 1937. But this, for Haro Ibars, was only a formal change. In 1979 he claimed to have become bored with the celebratory colourfulness of Madrid's carnival and to be feeling 'more and more depressed in this city', in which 'sex and drugs are badly regarded by all sectors of public and private opinion' (1979f).

As Haro Ibars put it, the rebels of his generation sought to escape their 'everyday life', which felt to them like an 'ill-air-conditioned nightmare', one day by using drugs to change their perception of reality, another day by thinking about ''Revolution', as a means to change the world, yet another day by following a guru who would suggest that the solution lied in 'meekness' and 'acceptance', only to end up 'bored with it all', seeking oblivion in alcohol and hard drugs (1979c). Among those who sought refuge in hard drugs and 'huge quantities of beer' were the so-called 'neo-existentialists', who 'vomited a lot' and tended to 'look around with the cold-fish expression typical of those who see the world as nonsensical folly' (1979d).

At the opposite end of the social spectrum were the teenagers and young people who joined the far-right organization *Cristo Rey* (Christ the King), responsible for acts of terrorism (including beating progressive priests in Ondarroa in 1970 and killing an anti-Franco demonstrator in 1976) and random attacks on civilians, like cutting men's long hair at gunpoint in a bar. Writing about such an attack in Madrid on the night of 27 February 1980, Haro Ibars concluded that 'far-right terrorists are bored and stupid, and also dangerous because they are allowed to be' (1980a).

In Spain in the late 1970s and early 1980s, one could hear an increasing number of expressions of tedium, boredom, existential boredom, uncertainty and dejection among the urbanites who had been born two to four decades earlier. They were disenchanted even with the new press: leftist and right-wing magazines were becoming 'increasingly tedious [*cada vez más aburridas*]'

(Haro Ibars, 1979b). It was that climate of disenchantment that the new adult comic strip magazines sought to capture and counteract. Inspired by the ways in which comic art had shaped North American society both as a commodity and as a new form in advertising (Gordon, 1998), they tried to shake and reshape post-Francoist Spanish society. For instance, *El Víbora. Comix contracultural* (1979–2004), influenced by North American underground comics (comix), presented itself in its first editorial as an 'attack against the crushing bores [*muermo*] and the piranhas, against the sleepiness of the survivors of this boring, authoritarian and, even worse, disjointed [*descangallada*] and stupid society' (1979). It depicted the 'underground' culture of the disenchanted, the 'couldn't-care-less' (*pasotas*), who had no political ideals. As Eduardo Subirats has noted, *pasotismo* was 'a true popular cultural current that broadly embraced the ethics of apathy and a kind of historical and social fatalism' (2005, p. 32). This ethics of apathy is captured in a remark made in 1983 by comic artist Montesol (Javier Ballester) about 'the countercultural-terrorist-druggy and abstentionist scene of *El Víbora,* which is going nowhere and has no way out' (cited in Pérez del Solar, 2013, p. 60). Disengaging from a society they found dull, *pasotas* tended to engage in ad-hoc activities, such as drug taking, which offered temporary escape from boredom, but which only served to intensify feelings of apathy and the sense of being stuck, of having nowhere to go.

At the start of 1980, Haro Ibars could only anticipate 'more years of boredom, of tedium, which we seek in vain to palliate with silly games, like children locked in their room without any toys', 'years of reading books that fail to interest, of watching expensive dull films, of going to concerts by incompetent bands' (1980b). A month later, the Canito Memorial concert, held in Madrid on 9 February, marked the beginning of the countercultural movement known as *movida,* which promoted a transgressive, moment-to-moment, party-animal existence. The Madrid *movida* is perhaps best known for its portrayal in the early films of Almodóvar, whose 'adolescent desire to shock implie[d] a desire to express what was previously repressed' (Wheeler, 2020, p. 185). It was also captured in the early photographs of Alberto García-Alix, displayed at the retrospective exhibition *Un Horizonte Falso* (A False Horizon) at the Maison Européenne de la Photographie in Paris in 2014, which showed 'needles going into veins, squalid flats, guns and knives and heedless sex and the pinched, anxious face of addiction' (Shinkle, 2015).

Was all that sex as meaningless as it now seems? Of course, what was/is fun to one person could be boring to others, as we can see from the claim made by Foucault when he was interviewed about his *History of Sexuality:* 'I must confess that I am much more interested in problems about techniques of the self and things like that rather than sex … sex is boring' (Dreyfus and Rabinow, 1983, p. 229). But for the protagonists of the *movida,* as for the Count Ory of the French medieval ballad or for Louis XV, sex was a way of combatting the tedium of life.

This was also the stated aim of the comic strip magazine *Cairo* (1981–1985), which, with its clear line style inspired by the Franco–Belgian juvenile comics of Hergé, addressed a fairly affluent young adult readership, providing them with 'a dose of adventures', so they could 'better evade the tedium of everyday reality' (*Cairo*, 1981). The magazine became the venue for black-and-white graphic-novel style comic strips like Montesol and Ramón de España's *La noche de siempre* (1981) and *Fin de Semana* (1982), which depicted the social practices of urban middle-class men and women in their twenties in Barcelona (the *movida barcelonesa*): alcohol, drugs, sex and discussions of cinema, art and music in the city's new 'modern' bars and clubs. But going out could also become tedious, as the text of the third vignette in Figure 22, from*Fin de*

Figure 22 'The same old bars', from 'Fin de semana', *Cairo,* 9 (1982).
© Montesol and Ramón de España

Figure 23 'Against Ibiza', from 'Fin de Semana', *Cairo,* 11 (1982), © Montesol
and Ramón de España

semana, suggests: 'Listen . . . if you don't mind, I would like to be taken home.
I am afraid I know what will happen tonight . . . Now we'll go to the same old
bars, to listen to the same old music and to talk to the same old people'
(Montesol and de España, 1982a).

To be sure, the *movida* was experienced differently by different groups of
people. For the reasonably well-off youngish Spaniards of the early 1980s, there
were a range of lifestyle options, evoked by the captions of Montesol and de
España's comic strip in Figure 23: 'Against Ibiza, Barcelona, Kathmandu,
New York, hippies, punks . . . the New Wave, politicians, Argentines, theatre
actors . . . radio programmes, bearded broadcasters, old friends, the past, the
present, the future, Amen' (Montesol and de España, 1982b). Here we see
a snapshot of the Spain of the early 1980s, in which one could be a hippy,
become a punk, lead one's life vicariously through the stimulation offered by
progressive radio broadcasters, or put one's act of being on hold by injecting
oneself with heroin. In 1982, when the consumption of heroin in Spain was
higher than in the United States (Usó, 2015, p. 127; cited in Wheeler, 2020,
p. 188), few people would find Kracauer's notion of *radikale Langeweile* an
attractive option.

A decade later, the writer and journalist Ignacio Vidal-Folch (born in 1956)
portrayed a former clandestine militant, named Wilhelm, who sought to alleviate his anxiety and sense of emptiness through compulsive shopping:

> I am a compulsive buyer – he confessed in an embarrassed voice – . When
> I find myself alone in the street, I feel fits of anguish. The world appears to me
> so empty . . . Then, in an attempt to alleviate my anxiety, I buy things, I buy all
> kinds of things I do not need until I am weighed down with ridiculous parcels,
> without a penny in my pocket, depressed. (1997, p. 88)

To some extent, the Spain of the 1990s can be described in the terms used by Brissett and Snow in relation to North America: 'the relative freedom from necessity, the growing reliance on consumer goods as ways of energizing ourselves, and the sense of liberation and emancipation felt by many Americans provide the conditions where boredom can so easily, and effortlessly, be experienced' (1993, p. 244). But Brisset and Snow go on to suggest that 'prior to the new comfort technology, mundane life was hard but not boring' (1993, p. 245), a statement that appears too simplistic in the light of the historical evidence I have discussed.

2.7 Global Boredom

In 1974–1976, a pioneering international collaborative study of male workers in Sweden concluded that perceived monotony at work was linked to a greater proneness to heart attacks, and to premature death due to cardiovascular disease (Alfredsson, Karasek and Theorell, 1982). These conclusions contrast with those of a more recent study by two British epidemiologists, which suggested that there is no demonstrable direct link between boredom and death, since factors such as employment circumstances, health and levels of physical activity play an important part (Britton and Shipley, 2010). In the meantime, however, newspapers and magazines have been drawing on snap-shot evidence from scientific studies, treating it as universal truths, and have been bombarding the general population with claims such as those made in the *Washington Post* in August 2005, that 'boredom is a condition that can be more stressful and damaging than overwork', and that it is rather widespread: 'we know that 55 percent of all U.S. employees are not engaged at work' (Joyce, 2005). While in the nineteenth century boredom had to do with the monotony of life, and in the early twentieth century it was also associated with mechanized jobs, in the twenty-first century 'the ever-burgeoning demands of meetings, paperwork, routinisation, information overload and bureaucracy within many job roles are creating a boom in the experience of workplace boredom' (Mann, 2007, p. 90; see also 2016). Boredom arises not only from having nothing to do, as in Figure 24, but also from the sense of having nowhere to go, as in the case of medical consultants who have reached their professional goals (Oxtoby, 2019).

Boredom has also been identified as one of the most pervasive and unpleasant emotions in school settings and the most prevalent negative emotion in univer-sities (e.g., Pekrun *et al.*, 2010; Nett, Goetz and Hall, 2011; Daschmann, Goetz and Stupnisky, 2014). When experienced in relation to achievement tasks in academic contexts, boredom often results in attention being withdrawn from

Figure 24 Agarwal and Baker, 'Yet another day to work on my nothing-to-do-list'. www.CartoonStock.com

Figure 25 Flavita Banana, Academic year 2020–2021: –'As a result of a world agreement, the subject of boredom will be part of this year's curriculum', 4 April 2020. © Flavia Álvarez / Ediciones El País S. L., 2020

activities which lack personal value, and directed towards stimuli and activities perceived to be more rewarding; it is associated with increased distractibility and a higher level of 'task-irrelevant thinking focused on alternative contents' (Pekrun *et al.*, 2010, p. 535). Boredom, alongside other negative emotions, such as hopelessness, has been found to decrease both intrinsic and extrinsic motivation, and to lead to shallow information-processing, rigid learning strategies and lower achievement (Pekrun *et al.*, 2002). There is ample scope for further analysis and discussion on how culture-specific teaching styles might be improved to increase motivation and reduce feelings of hopelessness and boredom. As Lucía Gómez and Francisco Jódar (2002) have noted in relation to the Spanish context, telling school children that they need to study now so as to 'become someone' in the future is not necessarily an effective way of counteracting their perception that schoolwork is boring, since it only serves to reinforce the impression that their present time is empty and devoid of meaning.

Meanwhile, it has become increasingly common to hear claims like 'let children get bored again' because boredom 'spawns creativity and self-sufficiency' and can thus lead to greater well-being (Paul, 2019). Such claims are in line with the views of a few researchers, who have emphasized the positive aspects of boredom, arguing that it promotes creativity (Mann and Cadman, 2014), that it 'encourages the behavioural pursuit of alternative goals' when current ones fail to satisfy (Bench and Lench, 2013), and that it can be considered as a regulatory state, directed at the pursuit of satisfactory activities (Danckert *et al.*, 2018b). Similarly, taking a functional approach, Elpidorou has seen boredom as the desire 'to be doing something else', and suggested that it 'informs us of our own goals, interests, and even self-perceived wellbeing' (2014, p. 2), and that it serves to 'promote well-being by contributing to personal growth and to the construction (or reconstruction) of a meaningful life' (2018b, p. 323), 'when the current goal ceases to be satisfactory, attractive, or meaningful' (2021b, p. 502).

There are a number of problems with such positive views of boredom. Firstly, it is only the situation that determines whether boredom is 'good' or 'bad'. As Wijnand van Tilburg points out, 'if a dull activity really needs to be done, then feeling bored is perhaps not very helpful' (Rhodes, 2015, p. 279). Secondly, as he also notes, even if boredom may 'serve an important psychological function' in that it 'makes people rethink what they are doing', choosing alternatives that seem more meaningful at that moment does not always bring about a positive change (p. 279).

Thirdly, functional views of boredom tend to focus on the potentially positive outcomes of escaping boredom, rather than on boredom itself. As Mark Kingwell reminds us, boredom should not be seen as a 'virtue' because it is 'unpleasant, enervating, frustrating and sometimes even immiserating' (2017, p. 231).

Fourthly, the desire to do something else is only one aspect of boredom, in itself not sufficient to bring about creativity, personal growth or well-being. Sometimes boredom cannot be explained as the effect of an external object or situation which might be replaced or changed, but depends on how one relates to that object or situation (as in the second and third types of boredom described by Heidegger).

Moreover, functional approaches tend to take no account of differences in the experience of boredom, its intensity, its duration, or its appropriateness in terms of longer-term goals. In arguing that boredom is a unitary construct, Elpidorou (2021b) does not consider how different degrees of boredom affect (and are affected by) one's general outlook on life. As Greenson (1951) noted when distinguishing between 'agitated' and 'apathetic' forms of boredom, the latter is associated with the tendency to perceive one's environment as dull and monotonous, and with a lack of desire to alter that experience.

When one is bored, one may experience a sense of disconnectedness and a diminished ability to care, which can make positive change more difficult. As Marco van Leewen suggests:

> I believe that boredom, in its essence, is about a failure to connect, about not fitting in, about not wanting or being able to interact. When we are bored, we cannot bring ourselves to care about something in particular (or anything at all), we do not feel that this thing that –or person who– we are confronted with is important enough to actually *connect* and *interact* with. (2009, p. 178)

The sense of disconnectedness associated with boredom can lead to carelessness as a mode of existence, as it did for the Spanish *pasotas* in the late 1970s and early 1980s. Carelessness might also manifest as acts of delinquency, which, according to recent sociological studies, can be seen as the 'creative' and 'exciting' ways in which some underprivileged young people seek to take control over their lives when they are bored with 'doing nothing' (Miller, 2005; Bengtsson, 2012).

It has even been suggested that youth unemployment, and the boredom it creates, is the main reason why foreign fighters from western countries such as Belgium, France, Germany, the United Kingdom and former Soviet republics like Russia, Kazakhstan and Uzbekistan join the Islamic State (Gouda and Marktanner, 2019). For those deprived of employment opportunities, or any satisfying activity in their home environments, becoming a fighter might seem attractive and meaningful.

Building on earlier research that indicated that proneness to boredom is a contributing factor in anger and aggression (Rupp and Vodanovich, 1997), a recent experimental study, in which the state of boredom was induced, led to the conclusion that when judging inter-group attacks, people who are bored are more lenient with members of their own cultural group and more severe with other cultural groups than people who are not bored (Van Tilburg and Igou, 2016). Nevertheless, these experiments can only identify short-term differences in perception, attributable to changes of mood induced in a lab, under controlled conditions. Their ecological validity is limited, and thus we should be careful not to extrapolate too much from their findings. Ultimately, it is difficult to prove scientifically the wide-picture observations made by social scientists, like Andrew Bowman, who claimed that 'ease engenders boredom and that boredom –unless otherwise assuaged – leads in the end to violence' (1975, p. 16).

The transient boredom that can be induced in a lab by making participants watch the same monotonous film clip repeatedly (Nederkoorn *et al.*, 2016) or read dull texts (Danckert *et al.*, 2018a) clearly differs from the ongoing (more chronic) type of boredom which researchers have identified as being often associated with drug and alcohol abuse (Iso-Ahola and Crowley, 1991; LePera, 2011; Weybright *et al.*, 2015), absenteeism from work, school or university, and with dropping out. The problem is that it is difficult to capture longer-term forms of boredom in a lab, or (as we have seen) through questionnaires.

Danckert and Eastwood have challenged the causal links that researchers have established between boredom and drugs or alcohol. They suggest that 'boredom doesn't directly make us drink or do drugs' and that these are simply forms of escapism: 'when we fail to exhibit any adaptive response, drugs and alcohol fill the gap by altering our mental state and ultimately numbing the negative feeling of boredom we want to escape' (2020, p. 95). Nonetheless, simple causal links still prevail among ordinary people.

For instance, in a study based on a sample of forty-three drug users aged twelve and below in Glasgow and Newcastle, James McIntosh and his colleagues offered evidence that even pre-teenagers who use recreational drugs justify their behaviour by saying that they are 'bored' and that taking drugs is 'fun': 'It's partly you're just bored. Nothing else to do. And it's fun. (Girl – aged 11)/ I used to do it all the time, every day nearly wi' ma cousin. Something to dae. Just bored man. (Boy – aged 12)' (2005, p. 39).

Even though not all the children in this study who claimed to be bored had taken drugs, the researchers concluded not only that 'boredom played a significant part in their drug-taking' and that 'feeling bored accentuated a child's curiosity to try new and potentially exciting things', but also that 'drug-taking itself provided something to do that was fun and socially bonding' (2005, p. 44). Since then, boredom has increasingly been seen as an excuse or an explanation for the rise in risk-taking activities among young people.

The label 'boredom' continues to be used to explain behaviours that can get 'out of hand', such as heavy drinking. For instance, in April 2020, during the first global Covid-19 lockdown, the number of people visiting the website of the charity Alcohol Change United Kingdom for help was up nearly 400 per cent, compared to the same period the previous year, and this raised concerns about possible 'long-term heavy drinking habits as a result of self-isolating at home'; people reported to be 'drinking more regularly out of "boredom" during the restrictions' (Lewis, 2020). In a web-based survey conducted by psychiatry researchers in Belgium during lockdown, boredom was also reported (alongside 'loneliness', 'lack of social contacts', 'loss of daily structure', 'reward after a hard-working day' and 'conviviality') as a reason for drinking and/or smoking more than before the pandemic (Vanderbruggen *et al.*, 2020).

Figure 26 Kostas Koufogiorgos, '– It is going to be a terribly boring winter. – That's really what I hope for myself . . .', 15 November 2020.
© Kostas Koufogiorgos

For Danckert and Eastwood, boredom both appeals to individual agency and limits it: 'to be bored is to be painfully stuck in the here and now, bereft of any capacity for self-determination, yet driven to find something that we can engage with' (2020, p. 19). Placing the focus on the individual, they see boredom as 'an experience occurring inside our minds' and 'part of our biology shaped by a long evolutionary heritage' (2020, pp. 3, 6). Perhaps it is time to take a wider perspective, and pay greater heed to the fact (demonstrated in my discussion of historical evidence and illustrated in Figures 5, 26 and 27) that many of the situations in which people have been bored or perceived to be bored are social situations.

In a recent, self-admittedly speculative, discussion of poverty and boredom, Elpidorou suggests that boredom is a more frequent and intense experience among people of low SES, who also find it more difficult to alleviate it, and are thus more likely to opt for maladaptive, even harmful responses than those of high SES. He claims that 'boredom is primarily the experience of the less privileged, the disadvantaged, and the marginalized' (2021a, p. 172). But when seeking to illustrate the impact of poverty on people's ability to endure boredom, he refers to a situation that is not necessarily the result of poverty:

> Students who are grappling with boredom while doing homework will be tempted to give it up and turn their attention to less effortful or more exciting projects to the detriment of their academic success, unless they have someone with them to help them with homework, instill in them the significance of doing homework, or motivate them to persist in their work. (pp. 189–90)

This example not only serves as a counterargument to Elpidorou's earlier claims about boredom as an adaptive mechanism. It also shows the importance of social environment in learning to endure boredom when needed. SES is an important factor when it comes to agency, but it does not determine whether or not people learn not to give up when something requires effort. The values of people who are present in our environment (be it a parent, a peer, a TV celebrity or an influencer) and the stories they tell us about what is relevant and meaningful or irrelevant and boring also have a significant influence.

Acknowledging some of the qualitative evidence of the diminished agency of bored individuals (e.g., Kanevsky and Keighley, 2003), Eastwood and Dana Gorelick (2021) also draw attention to the impact of structural forces on the experience of boredom. They make two important observations. Firstly, if you become aware that other people perceive what you do as having little value, you will be more likely to see your life as boring. Secondly, seeing the lives of people of higher SES may make you feel bored, if you live in underprivileged circumstances, lacking employment and education opportunities. Eastwood and

Gorelick conclude by warning that social inequalities can make disadvantaged people more vulnerable to chronic boredom.

Nonetheless, the observations made by Eastwood and Gorelick also provide evidence of the impact on the experience of boredom of other people's perceptions and of one's perceptions of others. Round the world, the global mass media are making people increasingly aware of inequalities, but also changing people's perceptions of what is meaningful and valuable. As Samuli Schielke notes in his study of rural Egypt, 'monotony as such does not necessarily bore people. It is turned into intense boredom and despair by the presence of strong but unfulfilled aspirations for a better and more exciting life' (2008, p. 251).

In the early 1990s, it was believed that boredom could be reduced by setting oneself challenges, by paying attention to sensory stimuli around oneself and by introducing some variety in the task (see, e.g., Sansone *et al.*, 1992). But now sensory stimulation, excitement and variety seem to be readily available through electronic devices which take attention away from our natural and social environment. It seems as if, at present, the fastest-growing form of

Figure 27 Ralph Ruthe, 'With this app, I can immediately know when I bore those around me. – Look! Now!', 30 January 2013.
© Ralph Ruthe

boredom is that which results from our 'failure' or 'unwillingness' to pay attention (Ringmar, 2017, p. 195). The speed at which we can move from one stimulus to another using modern technology is giving increasing prominence to feelings of disconnectedness and meaninglessness, associated with boredom.

Conclusion

The historical evidence I have discussed here challenges recent claims that boredom is a modern phenomenon, or that it appeared in the eighteenth century as a new concept. Boredom today, like in the past, is often the result of social interactions which are experienced as unpleasant (as in Montaigne), unsatisfying (Flaubert), flat and fleeting (Simmel), dull (Woolf), annoying (Lawrence), unfulfilling (as in Heidegger's example of the pleasant dinner party) or repetitive (as in Figure 22). What marks all such interactions (and those evoked in Figures 5 and 27) is that there is no mutual understanding or connectedness. This, as I have shown, is a common element in the experience of boredom across socio-historical contexts.

Different forms of boredom have coexisted within specific historical contexts. They have been shaped not only by economic and social circumstances, but also by the terms available to express and discuss them, and by the (social and textual) interactions that have given meaning to such terms. The terms, concepts and categories through which individuals have experienced their states of mind (and dispositions, such as melancholic temperament or 'boredom proneness') are culture-bound, but have also travelled across geographical and linguistic barriers, through translation, imitation and adaptation.

Just as the early modern term 'tediousness' evoked a range of interrelated feelings such as chagrin, displeasure, vexation, anger, grief, dismay, unease and annoyance, 'boredom' is also an umbrella term. It denotes a range of feelings and moods, from the short-term displeasure and annoyance experienced when disengaged and uninterested (e.g., when listening to seemingly irrelevant conversations, sermons or conference papers, or reading repetitive or unstimulating books) to complex longer-term states of mind (encompassing feelings of annoyance, worry, frustration, impotence and even despair), in situations perceived as unbearable, from which there appears to be no escape. These longer-term states of mind or moods include the saturation produced by excessive pleasure (evoked in the sixteenth century by the Latin *fastidium* and the English 'tediousness'), 'the restlessness of a vacant mind' (a phrase used by Johnson in 1759, rendered in the French translation as a particular state of *ennui*), and the chronic apathy or ennui that result from constant overstimulation (discussed by Simmel in 1903), as well as from the sustained failure to satisfy desires and from the satisfaction of all desires (Benon, 1939).

Long-term boredom, often experienced in constraining social circumstances, such as unemployment and enforced inactivity, cannot be reliably measured through quantitative studies. The weariness, hopelessness and despair of the *desoeuvré* in 1831 (depicted in Figure 13) clearly differ from the *ihbat* and *malal* of those interviewed by Schielke in the early twenty-first century, and from the despair of those who were deprived of work, social activities and freedom during the 2020 lockdowns. But, as the vignette in Figure 26 suggests, the experience of *Langeweile* also varies between people who interact within a particular sociocultural context, depending on their expectations (based on their prior experience).

The qualitative evidence offered by McIntosh and his colleagues supports the idea that boredom can be partly the result of social circumstances – the lack of age-appropriate things to do. But it also suggests that it is not simply drugs, but drug-taking as a social activity that can serve to distract young people from their perceived boredom. The intersubjective aspects of boredom and its antidotes are undeniable, and deserve further scholarly attention.

If we are constantly told that being busy and having access to more and more money (to be able to purchase exciting commodities and engage in endless stimulating activities) is the best form of existence, we may come to believe that spending time reflecting, studying, meditating or helping others is boring. While boredom sometimes arises from the mismatch between ability and level of difficulty (as Berlyne pointed out in 1960), it can also arise from a mismatch between duty and desire (as Fenichel noted in 1934). The more we hear (and tell ourselves) that satisfaction is to be found elsewhere, the more 'boring' our present tasks and situations will seem.

How many of us catch ourselves getting bored, or fed up, with trying to escape boredom, or the (perceived) monotony of our environment, by tapping on a screen and looking intently for something that can hold our attention, or inspire a new desire? More research is needed into the kind of strategies that can help us understand (and perhaps reduce) the feelings of boredom, frustration and annoyance that might arise when feeling 'stuck' (with nothing interesting to do), swamped (with monotonous work) or 'caught up' (in endless World Wide Web searches that bring no satisfaction).

Some of us have the option of seeing boredom as 'empty longing' (connecting with Schopenhauer or Greenson) or surrendering to the experience of slow time, *Langeweile* (with Kracauer). We might also understand (with Heidegger) the more profound *Langeweile* as a mood that enables deeper thinking, and might even choose to cultivate it (with Benjamin) as a state or relaxation and mental openness. Such intersubjective ways of understanding/experiencing

*"And this last chart illustrates why none of you
are here anymore. Questions?"*

Figure 28 Bradford Veley, '-And this last chart illustrates
why none of you are here anymore. Questions?'. www.CartoonStock.com

(*erfahren*) boredom should be further discussed, and be made more broadly available, beyond academia.

Paying attention to the diverse ways in which people have expressed, described and conceptualized boredom makes it possible to see it as more than an aversive state to be avoided, prevented, escaped or overcome. Reflecting on boredom (ours and that of other people, now and in the past) involves considering how the experience of feeling bored is shaped by circumstances, power relations and the rich nuances of the language available (beyond the keywords typically used in questionnaires). It can also involve crossing the epistemological and methodological boundaries between humanities and social science research to examine further the role of social interaction and of prevailing cultural values (including beliefs about gender and SES) in shaping the unfulfilled expectations that lie at the root of boredom.

References

ABC (1903) 'Tónico Koch', 12 March, p. 1.

Abramson, E. E. and Stinson, S. G. (1977) 'Boredom and Eating in Obese and Non-obese Individuals', *Addictive Behaviors*, 2(4), pp. 181–5.

Alfredsson, L., Karasek, R. and Theorell, T. (1982) 'Myocardial Infarction Risk and Psychosocial Work Environment: An Analysis of the Male Swedish Working Force', *Social Science & Medicine*, 16(4), pp. 463–7.

Baghdadchi, A. (2005) 'On Academic Boredom', *Arts and Humanities in Higher Education*, 4(3), pp. 319–24.

Barari, S., Caria, S., Davola, A. *et al.* (2020) 'Evaluating COVID-19 Public Health Messaging in Italy: Self-Reported Compliance and Growing Mental Health Concerns', *medRxiv* [Preprint]. www.medrxiv.org/content/10.1101/2020.03.27.20042820v2 (Accessed: 5 June 2020).

Barbalet, J. M. (1999) 'Boredom and Social Meaning', *The British Journal of Sociology*, 50(4), pp. 631–46.

Barbier, E. J. F. (1851) *Journal historique et anecdotique du règne de Louis XV*, vol. 3 (4 vol). Paris: Chapelet.

Barbier, E. J. F. (1856) *Journal historique et anecdotique du règne de Louis XV*, vol. 4 (4 vol). Paris: Chapelet.

Baudelaire, C. (1868) 'De l'essence du rire', in *Curiosités esthétiques*. Vol. II of *Œuvres complètes*. Paris: Michel Lévy frères, pp. 359–87.

Baudelaire, C. (2001) *Mon coeur mis à nu*. Edited by C. Pichois. Geneva: Droz.

Baum, M. (2020) *Die Hermeneutik Hans-Georg Gadamers als philosophia christiana*. Tübingen: Mohr Siebeck.

Bench, S. W. and Lench, H. C. (2013) 'On the Function of Boredom', *Behavioral Sciences*, 3(3), pp. 459–72.

Bengtsson, T. T. (2012) 'Boredom and Action – Experiences from Youth Confinement', *Journal of Contemporary Ethnography*, 41(5), pp. 526–53.

Benjamin, W. (1968) 'The Storyteller', in H. Arendt (ed.) *Illuminations: Essays and Reflections*. New York: Schocken Books, pp. 83–109.

Benjamin, W. (1991) 'Das Taschentuch', in R. Tiedemann and H. Schweppenhäuser (eds.) *Gesammelte Schriften*. Stuttgart: Suhrkap, p. 741.

Benjamin, W. (1999) *The Arcades Project*. Edited by H. Eiland and K. McLaughlin. Translated by R. Tiedemann. Cambridge, MA: Belknap Press of Harvard University Press.

Benon, R. (1939) 'Ennui et concupiscences. Ennui et asthénie', *Annales Médico-Psychologiques*, 97, Part 2, pp. 224–35.

Bentley, R. (1692) *A Confutation of Atheism from the Structure and Origin of Humane Bodies. A Sermon Preached at Saint Martin's in the Fields.* London: Printed for Henry Mortlock.

Berlyne, D. E. (1960) *Conflict, Arousal, and Curiosity.* New York: McGraw-Hill.

Bernstein, H. E. (1975) 'Boredom and the Ready-Made Life', *Social Research*, 42(3), pp. 512–37.

Bertrana, P. (1913) 'La esclavitut de l'homme de sa casa', *L'Esquella de la Torratxa*, 21 March, pp. 194–5.

Blumenberg, H. (2006) *Beschreibung des Menschen.* Frankfurt am Main: Suhrkamp.

Boden, J. (2009) 'The Devil Inside: Boredom Proneness and Impulsive Behaviour', in B. Dalle Pezze and C. Salzani (eds.) *Essays on boredom and Modernity.* Amsterdam: Rodopi, pp. 203–26.

Bourget, P. (1887) *Essais de psychologie contemporaine.* 5th ed. Paris: A. Lemerre.

Bowman, A. L. (1975) 'Poor, Nasty, Brutish and Short-But Seldom Boring', in F. R. Goetzl (ed.) *Boredom: Root of Discontent and Aggression.* Berkeley: Grizzly Peak Press pp. 11–33.

Brissett, D. and Snow, R. P. (1993) 'Boredom: Where the Future Isn't', *Symbolic Interaction*, 16(3), pp. 237–56.

Britton, A. and Shipley, M. J. (2010) 'Bored to Death?', *International Journal of Epidemiology*, 39(2), pp. 370–1.

Brodsky, J. (1995) 'In Praise of Boredom', in *On Grief and Reason: Essays.* New York: Farrar, Straus, Giroux, pp. 107–08.

Cairo (1981) 'Editorial', p. 1.

Campbell, J. (1989) *Joy in Work, German Work: The National Debate, 1800–1945.* Princeton, NJ: Princeton University Press.

Castillo, F. M. (1872) *Obras completas.* Mexico: Imprenta de la calle cerrada de Santa Teresa.

de Chenne, T. K. (1988) 'Boredom as a Clinical Issue', *Psychotherapy (Chicago, Ill.)*, 25(1), pp. 71–81.

Conrad, P. (1997) 'It's Boring: Notes on the Meanings of Boredom in Everyday Life', *Qualitative Sociology*, 20(4), pp. 465–75.

Cotgrave, R. (1611) *A Dictionarie of the French and English Tongues.* London: Adam Islip.

Covarrubias Orozco, S. de (1611) *Tesoro de la lengua castellana o española.* Madrid: Luis Sánchez.

Crockett, A. C., Myhre, S. K. and Rokke, P. D. (2015) 'Boredom Proneness and Emotion Regulation Predict Emotional Eating', *Journal of Health Psychology*, 20(5), pp. 670–80.

Csikszentmihalyi, M. (1975) *Beyond Boredom and Anxiety*. San Francisco: Jossey-Bass.

Csikszentmihalyi, M. (1997) *Finding Flow: The Psychology of Engagement with Everyday Life*. New York: Basic Books.

Dalle Pezze, B. and Salzani, C. (eds.) (2009) *Essays on Boredom and Modernity*. Amsterdam: Rodopi.

Danckert, J., Hammerschmidt, T., Marty-Dugas, J. and Smilek, D. (2018a) 'Boredom: Under-Aroused and Restless', *Consciousness and Cognition*, 61, pp. 24–37.

Danckert, J., Mugon, J., Struk, A. and Eastwood, J. (2018b) 'Boredom: What Is It Good for?', in H. C. Lench (ed.) *The Function of Emotions: When and Why Emotions Help Us*. Cham: Springer, pp. 93–119.

Danckert, J. and Eastwood, J. D. (2020) *Out of My Skull: The Psychology of Boredom*. Cambridge, MA: Harvard University Press.

Darden, D. K. (1999) 'Boredom: A Socially Disvalued Emotion', *Sociological Spectrum*, 19(1), pp. 13–37.

Daschmann, E. C., Goetz, T. and Stupnisky, R. H. (2014) 'Exploring the Antecedents of Boredom: Do Teachers Know Why Students are Bored?', *Teaching and Teacher Education*, 39, pp. 22–30.

Davies, A. H. (1926) 'Discussion on the Physical and Mental Effects of Monotony in Modern Industry', *The British Medical Journal*, 2(3427), pp. 472–79.

Delacroix, E. (1893) *Journal*. Edited by P. Flat and R. Piot. Paris: Plon.

Dexter, E. S. (1935) 'The Effect of Fatigue or Boredom on Teachers' Marks', *The Journal of Educational Research*, 28, pp. 664–7.

Dictionnaire de l'Académie françoise. 3rd ed. (1740). Paris: Jean-Baptiste Coignard.

Diderot, D. (1748) *Les Bijoux indiscrets* (2 vol). Monomotapa [Paris].

Diderot, D. (1749) *Les Bijoux indiscrets. Or, the Indiscreet Toys. Translated from the Congese language*. Tobago: Pierrot Ragout.

Doehlemann, M. (1991) *Langeweile? Deutung eines verbreiteten Phänomens*. Frankfurt am Main: Suhrkamp.

Dreyfus, H. L. and Rabinow, P. (1983) *Michel Foucault: Beyond Structuralism and Hermeneutics*. 2nd ed. Chicago: University of Chicago Press.

Dumonceaux, P. (1975) *Langue et sensibilité au XVIIe siècle: L'évolution du vocabulaire affectif*. Geneva: Droz.

Dupuis, L. (1922) 'L'ennui morbide', *Revue philosophique de la France et de l'étranger*, 93, pp. 417–42.

Eastwood, J. D., Cavaliere, C., Fahlman, S. A., Eastwood, A. E. (2007) 'A Desire for Desires: Boredom and Its Relation to Alexithymia', *Personality and Individual Differences*, 42(6), pp. 1035–45.

Eastwood, J. D., Frischen, A., Fenske, M. J. and Smilek, D. (2012) 'The Unengaged Mind: Defining Boredom in Terms of Attention', *Perspectives on Psychological Science*, 7(5), pp. 482–95.

Eastwood, J. D. and Gorelick, D. (2021) 'Losing and Finding Agency: The Crisis of Boredom', in A. Elpidorou (ed.) *The Moral Psychology of Boredom*. Lanham: Rowman & Littlefield, pp. 111–31.

Ekman, P. (1993) 'Facial Expression and Emotion', *American Psychologist*, 48, pp. 384–92.

El Grito Arjentino (1839), 24 February.

El Liberal (1900) 'Tónico Koch', 24 June, p. 4.

El Víbora. Comix contracultural (1979) 'Editorial', p. 3.

Elpidorou, A. (2014) 'The Bright Side of Boredom', *Frontiers in Psychology*, 5 (art. 1245), pp. 1–4.

Elpidorou, A. (2015) 'The Significance of Boredom: A Sartrean Reading', in D. O. Dahlstrom, A. Elpidorou, and W. Hopp (eds.) *Philosophy of Mind and Phenomenology: Conceptual and Empirical Approaches*. New York: Routledge (Routledge Research in Phenomenology), pp. 268–83.

Elpidorou, A. (2018a) 'The Bored Mind is a Guiding Mind: Toward a Regulatory Theory of Boredom', *Phenomenology and the Cognitive Sciences*, 17(3), pp. 455–84.

Elpidorou, A. (2018b) 'The Good of Boredom', *Philosophical Psychology*, 31 (3), pp. 323–51.

Elpidorou, A. (2021a) 'Boredom and Poverty: A Theoretical Model', in A. Elpidorou (ed.) *The Moral Psychology of Boredom*. Lanham: Rowman & Littlefield, pp. 171–208.

Elpidorou, A. (2021b) 'Is Boredom One or Many? A Functional Solution to the Problem of Heterogeneity', *Mind & Language*, 36(3), pp. 491–511.

Elpidorou, A. (2021c) 'The Moral Significance of Boredom: An Introduction', in A. Elpidorou (ed.) *The Moral Psychology of Boredom*. Lanham: Rowman & Littlefield, pp. 1–33.

Elyot, T. (1538) *The Dictionary of syr Thomas Eliot knyght*. London: Thomas Berthelet.

Epstein, J. (2012) 'Duh, Bor-ing', in R. Atwan (ed.) *The Best American Essays 2012*. Boston: Houghton Mifflin Harcourt, pp. 102–10.

Fahlman, S. A., Mercer-Lynn, K. B., Flora, D. B. and Eastwood, J. D. (2013) 'Development and Validation of the Multidimensional State Boredom Scale', *Assessment*, 20(1), pp. 68–85.

Farmer, R. and Sundberg, N. D. (1986) 'Boredom Proneness –The Development and Correlates of a New Scale', *Journal of Personality Assessment*, 50(1), pp. 4–17.

Fenichel, O. (1951) 'On the Psychology of Boredom', in D. Rapaport, *Organization and Pathology of Thought*: Selected Sources. New York: Columbia University Press, pp. 329–61.

Fenichel, O. (1953) 'On the Psychology of Boredom', in H. Fenichel and D. Rapaport (eds.) *The Collected Papers of Otto Fenichel. First Series*. New York: W. W. Norton, pp. 292–302.

Fernández, J. J. (1977) 'Editorial', *Star*, June, p. 4.

Fernandez, L. and Matt, S. J. (2019) *Bored, Lonely, Angry, Stupid: Changing Feelings about Technology, from the Telegraph to Twitter*. Cambridge, MA: Harvard University Press.

Fisher, C. D. (1993) 'Boredom at Work: A Neglected Concept', *Human Relations*, 46(3), pp. 395–417.

Flaubert, G. (1988) *Carnets de travail*. Edited by P.-M. de Biasi. Paris: Balland.

Flaubert, G. (2001) *Correspondance. Tome I: Du College a L'Orient (1830–1851)*. Edited by G. Bonaccorso. Saint-Genouph: NIzet.

Gadamer, H.-G. (2004) *Truth and Method*. 2nd revised ed. Translated by J. Weinsheimer and D. G. Marshall. London: Continuum.

Gergen, K. J. (2015) *An Invitation to Social Construction*. 3rd ed. London: Sage.

Gómez, L. and Jódar, F. J. (2002) 'Escuela, aburrimiento y rebeldía', *Athenea digital*, 1(2), pp. 18–29.

Goodstein, E. S. (2005) *Experience without Qualities: Boredom and Modernity*. Stanford, CA: Stanford University Press.

Goodstein, E. S. (2020) 'Boredom and the Disciplinary Imaginary', in J. Ros Velasco (ed.) *The Culture of Boredom*. Leiden: Brill (Critical Studies, 40), pp. 23–54.

Gordon, I. (1998) *Comic Strips and Consumer Culture, 1890–1945*. Washington, DC: Smithsonian Institution Press.

Gouda, M. and Marktanner, M. (2019) 'Muslim Youth Unemployment and Expat Jihadism: Bored to Death?', *Studies in Conflict & Terrorism*, 42(10), pp. 878–97.

Greenson, R. R. (1951) 'Apathetic and Agitated Boredom', *Psychoanalytical Quarterly*, 20, pp. 346–47.

Greenson, R. R. (1953) 'On boredom', *Journal of the American Psychoanalytic Association*, 1(1), pp. 7–21.

Griffiths, P. E. and Scarantino, A. (2009) 'Emotions in the Wild: The Situated Perspective on Emotion', in P. Robbins and M. Ayedede (eds.) *The Cambridge Handbook of Situated Cognition*. Cambridge: Cambridge University Press.

Grose, F. (1785) *Classical Dictionary of the Vulgar Tongue*. London: S. Hooper.

Habermas, J. (1984) *The Theory of Communicative Action: Reason and the Rationalization of Society*. London: Heinemann.

Hacker, P. M. S. (2012) 'The Relevance of Wittgenstein's Philosophy of Psychology to the Psychological Sciences', in P. Stekeler-Weithofer (ed.) *Wittgenstein: Zu Philosophie und Wissenschaft*. Hamburg: Felix Meiner, pp. 205–23.

Haladyn, J. J. (2015) *Boredom and Art: Passions of the Will to Boredom*. Alresford: Zero Books.

Hamilton, J. A., Haier, R. J. and Buchsbaum, M. S. (1984) 'Intrinsic Enjoyment and Boredom Coping Scales: Validation with Personality, Evoked Potential and Attention Measures', *Personality and Individual Differences*, 5(2), pp. 183–93.

Hammer, E. (2004) 'Being Bored: Heidegger on Patience and Melancholy', *British Journal for the History of Philosophy*, 12(2), p. 277.

Hardy, T. (1876) *The Hand of Ethelberta: A Comedy in Chapters*. New York: H. Holt.

Haro Ibars, E. (1976) 'La revolución mística de André Bretón', *Tiempo de Historia*, 1 October, pp. 72–82.

Haro Ibars, E. (1977) 'La Generación del 27: Todo el espíritu de una época', *Tiempo de Historia*, 1 September, pp. 38–47.

Haro Ibars, E. (1979a) 'Cultura a la contra: Barrios y ciudad', *Triunfo*, 21 July, p. 48.

Haro Ibars, E. (1979b) 'Cultura a la contra: Contra todo', *Triunfo*, 6 October, p. 50.

Haro Ibars, E. (1979c) 'Cultura a la contra: Encantamiento', *Triunfo*, 7 April, p. 58.

Haro Ibars, E. (1979d) 'Cultura a la contra: Los nuevos hippies', *Triunfo*, 27 October, p. 58.

Haro Ibars, E. (1979e) 'Cultura a la contra: Primavera', *Triunfo*, 5 May, p. 54.

Haro Ibars, E. (1979f) 'Cultura a la contra: Punks y punkettes, salid de vuestras alcantarillas', *Triunfo*, 1 March, p. 48.

Haro Ibars, E. (1979g) 'La homosexualidad como problema socio-político en el cine español del postfranquismo (o como aprendí a dejar atrás toda esperanza al penetrar en un cine)', *Tiempo de Historia*, 1 March, pp. 88–91.

Haro Ibars, E. (1980a) 'Cultura a la contra: Aburridos, pesados terroristas', *Triunfo*, 12 January, p. 50.

Haro Ibars, E. (1980b) 'Cultura a la contra: Los pasos perdidos', *Triunfo*, 5 January, p. 50.

Harris, M.B. (2000) 'Correlates and Characteristics of Boredom Proneness and Boredom', *Journal of Applied Social Psychology*, 30, pp. 576–98.

Harrison, L. (1571) *A Dictionarie French and English*. London: Henry Bynneman.

Healy, S. D. (1984) *Boredom, Self, and Culture*. Cranbury, NJ: Associated University Presses.

Hebb, D. O. (1966) *A Textbook of Psychology*. 2nd ed. London: W. B. Saunders.

Heidegger, M. (1983) *Grundbegriffe der Metaphysik. Welt – Endlichkeit – Einsamkeit*. Edited by F. W. von Herrmann. Frankfurt am Main: Vittorio Klostermann.

Heidegger, M. (1995) *The Fundamental Concepts of Metaphysics: World, Finitude, Solitude*. Translated by W. McNeill and N. Walker. Bloomington, IN: Indiana University Press.

Horwicz, A. (1875) *Psychologische Analysen auf Physiologischer Grundlage*. Halle: C. E. M. Pfeffer.

Huguet, M. (1984) *L'ennui et ses discours*. Paris: Presses Universitaires de France.

Hunter, J. A., Dyer, K. J., Cribbie, R. A. and Eastwood, J. D. (2016) 'Exploring the Utility of the Multidimensional State Boredom Scale', *European Journal of Psychological Assessment: Official Organ of the European Association of Psychological Assessment*, 32(3), pp. 241–50.

Isabelle, A. (1835) *Voyage à Buénos-Ayres et à Porto-Alègre, par la Banda-oriental, les missions d'Uruguay et la province de Rio-Grande-do-Sul, de 1830 à 1834*. Havre: J. Morlent.

Iso-Ahola, S. E. and Crowley, E. D. (1991) 'Adolescent Substance Abuse and Leisure Boredom', *Journal of Leisure Research*, 23(3), pp. 260–71.

Iso-Ahola, S. E. and Weissinger, E. (1990) 'Perceptions of Boredom in Leisure: Conceptualization, Reliability and Validity of the Leisure Boredom Scale', *Journal of Leisure Research*, 22(1), pp. 1–17.

James, W. (1886) 'The Perception of Time', *The Journal of Speculative Philosophy*, 20(4), pp. 374–407.

James, W. (1890) *The Principles of Psychology*. New York: Henry Holt and Company.

Jaucourt, M. L. C. de (1755) 'Ennui', in D. Diderot and J. le Rond D'Alembert (eds.) *Encyclopédie ou dictionnaire raisonné des sciences, des arts et des métiers*. Paris: Briasson-David-Le Breton-Durand.

Johnson, S. (1755) *A Dictionary of the English Language*. London: Printed by W. Strahan, for J. & P. Knapton.

Johnson, S. (1790) *Le Paresseux*. Translated by J.-B. Varney. Paris: Maradan.

Johnson, S. (1834) *The Works of Samuel Johnson*, vol. 1. Edited by A. Murphy. New York: George Dearborn.

Johnson, S. (1854) *The Works of Samuel Johnson*, vol. 2. Edited by A. Murphy. London: Henry G. Bohn.

Joyce, A. (2005) 'Boredom Numbs the Work World', *The Washington Post*, 10 August. www.washingtonpost.com/wpdyn/content/article/2005/08/09/ AR2005080901395.html [accessed: 23 May 2020].

Kagan, J. (2007) *What is Emotion? History, Measures, and Meanings*. New Haven: Yale University Press.

Kaiser, T. E. (1996) 'Madame de Pompadour and the Theaters of Power', *French Historical Studies*, 19(4), pp. 1025–44.

Kanevsky, L. and Keighley, T. (2003) 'To Produce or Not to Produce? Understanding Boredom and the Honor in Underachievement', *Roeper Review*, 26(1), pp. 20–28.

Kessel, M. (2001) *Langeweile: Zum Umgang mit Zeit und Gefühlen in Deutschland vom späten 18. bis zum frühen 20. Jahrhundert*. Göttingen: Wallstein Verlag.

Kierkegaard, S. (1987) *Either/Or, Part. I*. Translated by H. Hong and E. Hong. Princeton, NJ: Princeton University Press.

Kingwell, M. (2017) 'Boredom and the Origin of Philosophy', in M. E. Gardiner and J. J. Haladyn (eds.) *Boredom Studies Reader: Frameworks and Perspectives*. Abingdon: Routledge, pp. 216–33.

Klapp, O. E. (1986) *Overload and Boredom: Essays on the Quality of Life in the Information Society*. New York: Greenwood Press.

Kracauer, S. (1995) 'Boredom', in T. Y. Levin (ed. and tran.) *The Mass Ornament: Weimar Essays*. Cambridge, MA: Harvard University Press, pp. 331–4.

Kuhn, R. (1976) *The Demon of Noontide: Ennui in Western Literature*. Princeton, NJ: Princeton University Press.

Lacroix, P. (1830) 'Longchamps', *Le Gastronome: Journal Universel du goût, rédigé par une société d'hommes de bouche et d'hommes de lettres*, 11 April, pp. 4–5.

Lafont, C. (1999) *The Linguistic Turn in Hermeneutic Philosophy*. Translated by J. Medina. Cambridge, MA, : MIT Press.

Laplana, J. de C. (1995) *Santiago Rusiñol: el pintor, l'home*. Barcelona: Abadia de Montserrat.

Lawrence, D. H. (2002) *Lady Chatterley's Lover and A Propos of 'Lady Chatterley's Lover'*. Edited by M. Squires. Cambridge: Cambridge University Press.

Le Savoureux, H. (1913) *Le spleen*. Paris: Steinheil.

Le Savoureux, H. (1914) 'L'Ennui normal et l'ennui morbide', *Journal de Psychologie normale et pathologique*, 10, pp. 131–48.

Lee, T. W. (1986) 'Toward the Development and Validation of a Measure of Job Boredom', *Manhattan College Journal of Business*, 15, pp. 22–8.

Leeuwen, M. van (2009) 'The Digital Void: e-NNUI and Experience', in B. Dalle Pezze and C. Salzani (eds.) *Essays on Boredom and Modernity.* Amsterdam: Rodopi, pp. 177–201.

Lelia (1879) 'Modas', *La Ondina del Plata*, 23 February, 5(8), pp. 90–2.

Lennox, S. (1901) *The Life and Letters of Lady Sarah Lennox, 1745–1826.* Edited by C. of Ilchester. London: John Murray.

LePera, N. (2011) 'The Relationships between Boredom Proneness, Mindfulness, Anxiety, Depression, and Substance Use', *The New School Psychology Bulletin*, 8(2), pp. 15–25.

L'Esquella de la Torratxa (1916) 'Polèmica de carnaval', 3 March, p. 153.

Lewinsky, H. (1943) 'Boredom', *British Journal of Educational Psychology*, 13, pp. 147–52.

Lewis, T. (2020) 'Coronavirus: Alcohol Fears Amid Lockdown Boredom', *BBC News*, 28 April. www.bbc.co.uk/news/uk-wales-52442936 (Accessed: 22 May 2020).

Littré, É. (1863) *Dictionnaire de la langue française.* Paris: Librairie de L. Hachette et Cie.

Los Deportes (Bilbao) (1916), 22 June.

MacIntyre, A. (1981) *After Virtue.* Notre Dame, IN: University of Notre Dame Press.

Malpas, J. and Zabala, S. (eds.) (2010) *Consequences of Hermeneutics: Fifty Years after Gadamer's Truth and Method.* Evanston, IL: Northwestern University Press.

Mann, S. (2007) 'The Boredom Boom'', *The Psychologist*, 20(2) pp. 90–3.

Mann, S. (2016) *The Upside of Downtime: Why Boredom is Good.* London: Robinson.

Mann, S. and Cadman, R. (2014) 'Does Being Bored Make Us More Creative?', *Creativity Research Journal*, 26(2), pp. 165–73.

Mantegazza, P. (1867) *Fisiologia del piacere.* MIlan: G. Bernardoni.

Markey, A., Chin, A., Vanepps, E. M. and Loewenstein, G. (2014) 'Identifying a Reliable Boredom Induction', *Perceptual and Motor Skills*, 119(1), pp. 237–53.

Martin, M., Sadlo, G. and Stew, G. (2006) 'The Phenomenon of Boredom', *Qualitative Research in Psychology*, 3(3), pp. 193–211.

Mascolo, M. F. (2009) 'Wittgenstein and the Discursive Analysis of Emotion', *New Ideas in Psychology*, 27(2), pp. 258–74.

Mascolo, M. F. and Kallio, E. (2020) 'The Phenomenology of Between: An Intersubjective Epistemology for Psychological Science', *Journal of Constructivist Psychology*, 33(1), pp. 1–28.

McIntosh, J., MacDonald, F. and McKeganey, N. (2005) 'Pre-teenage Children's Experiences of Drug Use', *International Journal of Drug Policy*, 16(1), pp. 37–45.

Mercer, K. B. and Eastwood, J. D. (2010) 'Is Boredom Associated with Problem Gambling Behaviour? It Depends on What You Mean by "Boredom"', *International Gambling Studies*, 10(1), pp. 91–104.

Mercer-Lynn, K. B., Bar, R. J. and Eastwood, J. D. (2014) 'Causes of Boredom: The Person, the Situation, or Both?', *Personality and Individual Differences*, 56, pp. 122–6.

Mercer-Lynn, K. B., Flora, D. B., Fahlman, S. A. and Eastwood, J. D. (2013a) 'The Measurement of Boredom: Differences between Existing Self-Report Scales', *Assessment*, 20(5), pp. 585–96.

Mercer-Lynn, K. B., Hunter, J. A. and Eastwood, J. D. (2013b) 'Is Trait Boredom Redundant?', *Journal of Social and Clinical Psychology*, 32(8), pp. 897–916.

Meumann, E. (1894) 'Untersuchungen zur Psychologie und Aesthetik des Rhythmus', *Philosophische Studien*, 10, pp. 249–322, 393–430.

Miller, W. (2005) 'Adolescents on the Edge: The Sensual Side of Delinquency', in S. Lyng (ed.) *Edgework: The Sociology of Risk-Taking*. New York: Routledge, pp. 153–71.

Montaigne, M. de (1588) *Essais*. Paris: Abel L'Angelier.

Montaigne, M. de (1613) *Essayes*. Translated by J. Florio. London: Printed by Melch. Bradvvood for Edvvard Blount and William Barret.

Montaigne, M. de (1685) *Essays of Michael, seigneur de Montaigne*. Translated by C. Cotton. London: Printed for T. Basset, M. Gilliflower and W. Hensman.

Montaigne, M. de (1965) *Essais*. Edited by P. Villey and V.-L. Saulnier. Paris: PUF.

Montesol and de España, R. (1982a) 'Fin de semana', *Cairo*, p. 42.

Montesol and de España, R. (1982b) 'Fin de semana', *Cairo*, p. 48.

Montesquieu, C. L. de S. de M. (1736) *Persian Letters*. 3rd ed. Translated by Ozell. London: J. Tonson.

Moynihan, A. B., van Tilburg, W. A. P., Igou, E. R. *et al.* (2015) 'Eaten Up by Boredom: Consuming Food to Escape Awareness of the Bored Self', *Frontiers in Psychology*, 6, pp. 1–10.

Münsterberg, H. (1913) 'Experiments on the Problem of Monotony', in *Psychology and Industrial Efficiency*. Boston: Houghton Mifflin Harcourt.

Musharbash, Y. (2007) 'Boredom, Time, and Modernity: An Example from Aboriginal Australia', *American Anthropologist*, 109(2), pp. 307–17.

Nederkoorn, C., Vancleef, L., Wilkenhöner, A., Claes, L. and Havermans, R. C. (2016) 'Self-Inflicted Pain out of Boredom', *Psychiatry Research*, 237, pp. 127–32.

Nett, U. E., Goetz, T. and Hall, N. C. (2011) 'Coping with Boredom in School: An Experience Sampling Perspective', *Contemporary Educational Psychology*, 36(1), pp. 49–59.

Ng, A. H., Liu, Y., Chen, J. and Eastwood, J. D. (2015) 'Culture and State Boredom: A Comparison between European Canadians and Chinese', *Personality and Individual Differences*, 75, pp. 13–18.

Ngai, S. (2008) 'Merely Interesting', *Critical Inquiry*, 34(4), pp. 777–817.

Nicot, J. (1606) *Thresor de la langue françoyse*. Paris: David Douceur.

Nietzsche, F. (2012) *Human, All Too Human*. Translated by H. Zimmern and P. V. Cohn. Mineola, NY: Dover.

Nuevo Mundo (1909a) 'La enfermedad del siglo', 18 February, p. 24.

Nuevo Mundo (1909b) 'Tónico Koch', 18 February, p. 2.

OED (2020). www-oed-com (Accessed: 16 June 2020).

Ohlmeier, S., Finkielsztein, M. and Pfaff, H. (2020) 'Why We are Bored: Towards a Sociological Approach to Boredom', *Sociological Spectrum*, 40 (3), pp. 208–25.

Ortony, A., Clore, G. L. and Collins, A. (1988) *The Cognitive Structure of Emotions*. Cambridge: Cambridge University Press.

Overgaard, S. (2006) 'The Problem of Other Minds: Wittgenstein's Phenomenological Perspective', *Phenomenology and the Cognitive Sciences*, 5 (1), pp. 53–73.

Oxtoby, K. (2019) 'How Not to Get Bored Mid-Career', *British Medical Journal*, 365(12274), pp. 1–2.

Palencia, A. de (1490) *Universal vocabulario en latin y en romance o Universale compendium vocabulorum cum vulgari expositione*. Seville: Paulus de Colonia, Johannes Pegnitzer, Magnus Herbst and Thomas Glockner.

Palerm, E. (2016) 'Aspectes contratransferencials de la somnolència i l'avorriment', *Revista Catalana de Psicoanàlisi*, 33(2), pp. 7–23.

Paliwoda, D. (2010) *Melville and the Theme of Boredom*. Jefferson, MO: McFarland & Company.

Palsgrave, J. (1530) *Lesclarcissement de la langue francoyse* London: R. Pynson and J. Haukyns.

Paul, P. (2019) 'Let Children Get Bored Again', *The New York Times*, 2 February. www.nytimes.com/2019/02/02/opinion/sunday/children-bored.html (Accessed: 31 May 2020).

Payot, J. (1901) *La educación de la voluntad*. 2nd ed. Translated by M. Antón y Ferrándiz. Madrid: Fernando Fe.

Pease, A. (2012) *Modernism, Feminism and the Culture of Boredom.* Cambridge: Cambridge University Press.

Pedretti, (2013) 'Late Modern Rigmarole: Boredom as Form in Samuel Beckett's Trilogy', *Studies in the Novel*, 45(4), pp. 583–602.

Pekrun, R., Goetz, T., Titz, W. and Perry, R. P. (2002) 'Academic Emotions in Students' Self-Regulated Learning and Achievement: A Program of Qualitative and Quantitative Research', *Educational Psychologist*, 37(2), pp. 91–105.

Pekrun, R., Daniels, L. M., Goetz, T., Stupnisky, R. H. and Perry, R. P. (2010) 'Boredom in Achievement Settings: Exploring Control-Value Antecedents and Performance Outcomes of a Neglected Emotion', *Journal of Educational Psychology*, 102(3), pp. 531–49.

Percy, W. (1958) 'Symbol, Consciousness, and Intersubjectivity', *The Journal of Philosophy*, 55(15), pp. 631–41.

Pérez, D. (1909) 'Menos música', *Nuevo Mundo*, 21 January, p. 4.

Pérez del Solar, P. (2013) *Imágenes del desencanto: Nueva historieta española 1980–1986*. Frankfurt am Main: Vervuert (La Casa de la Riqueza. Estudios de la Cultura de España).

Peters, E. (1975) 'Notes toward an Archaeology of Boredom', *Social Research*, 42(3), pp. 493–511.

Phiddian, R. (2020) *Satire and the Public Emotions*. Cambridge: Cambridge University Press.

Phillips, A. (1993) 'On Being Bored', in *On Kissing, Tickling and Being Bored: Psychoanalytic Essays on the Unexamined Life*. Cambridge, MA: Harvard University Press, pp. 68–78.

Phillips, J. (2004) 'Beckett's Boredom and the Spirit of Adorno', *Samuel Beckett Today/Aujourd'hui*, 14, pp. 251–9.

Plutchik, R. (1962) *The Emotions: Facts, Theories and a New Model.* New York: Crown Publishing Group/Random House (The emotions: Facts, theories and a new model.), pp. viii, 204.

Racker, H. (1957) 'The Meanings and Uses of Countertransference', *The Psychoanalytic Quarterly*, 26(3), pp. 303–57.

Racker, H. (2007) 'The Meanings and Uses of Countertransference', *The Psychoanalytic Quarterly*, 76(3), pp. 725–77.

Ragheb, M. G. and Merydith, S. P. (2001) 'Development and Validation of a Multidimensional Scale Measuring Free Time Boredom', *Leisure Studies*, 20(1), pp. 41–59.

Raposa, M. (1999) *Boredom and the Religious Imagination*. Charlottesville, VA: University of Virginia Press.

Razzell, P. and Spence, C. (2007) 'The History of Infant, Child and Adult Mortality in London, 1550–1850', *The London Journal*, 32(3), pp. 271–92.

Reddy, W. M. (1997) 'Against Constructionism: The Historical Ethnography of Emotions', *Current Anthropology*, 38(3), pp. 327–51.

Reddy, W. M. (2001) *The Navigation of Feeling: A Framework for the History of Emotions*. Cambridge: Cambridge University Press.

Rhodes, E. (2015) 'The Exciting Side of Boredom', *The Psychologist*, April, pp. 278–81.

Ringmar, E. (2017) 'Attention and the Cause of Modern Boredom', in M. E. Gardiner and J. J. Haladyn (eds.) *Boredom Studies Reader: Frameworks and Perspectives*. Abingdon: Routledge, pp. 193–202.

Rock, D. (2018) *The British in Argentina: Commerce, Settlers and Power, 1800–2000*. Basingstoke: Palgrave Macmillan.

Ros Velasco, J. (2021) 'The Long Hard Road Out of Boredom', in A. Elpidorou (ed.) *The Moral Psychology of Boredom*. Lanham: Rowman & Littlefield, pp. 291–311.

Ros Velasco, J. (2022) *La enfermedad del aburrimiento*. Madrid: Alianza.

Rosen, C. (2012) *Freedom and the Arts: Essays on Music and Literature*. Cambridge, MA: Harvard University Press.

Rossi, R. (2018) 'Writing Disgust, Writing Realities: The Complexity of Negative Emotions in Émile Zola's *Nana*', in I. Jandl, S. Knaller, S. Schönefellner and G. Trockner (eds.) *Writing Emotions: Theoretical Concepts and Selected Case Studies in Literature*. Bielefeld: Transcript-Verlag (Lettre), pp. 277–93.

Roy, A. and Oludaja, B. (2009) 'Hans-Georg Gadamer's Praxis: Implications for Connection and Action in Communication Studies', *Communication, Culture & Critique*, 2(3), pp. 255–73.

Rupp, D. E. and Vodanovich, S. J. (1997) 'The Role of Boredom Proneness in Self-Reported Anger and Aggression', *Journal of Social Behavior and Personality*, 12(4), pp. 925–36.

Rusiñol, S. (1947) *Obres Completes*. Barcelona: Selecta.

Salzani, C. (2009) 'The Atrophy of Experience: Walter Benjamin and Boredom', in B. Dalle Pezze and C. Salzani (eds.) *Essays on Boredom and Modernity*. Amsterdam: Rodopi, pp. 127–54.

Sansone, C., Weir, C., Harpster, L. and Morgan, C. (1992) 'Once a Boring Task Always a Boring Task? Interest as a Self-Regulatory Mechanism', *Journal of Personality and Social Psychology*, 63(3), pp. 379–90.

Sarría Buil, A. (2015) 'Cultura y memoria "a la contra". Estudio', in Haro Ibars, E., *Cultura y memoria 'a la contra'. Artículos en las revistas Triunfo y Tiempo de Historia (1975–1982)*. Edited by A. Sarría Buil. Madrid: Postmetropolis Editorial, pp. i–lxxxvi.

Sartre, J.-P. (1947) *Existentialism*. Translated by B. Frechtman. New York: Philosophical Library.

Scherer, K. R. (2005) 'What are Emotions? And How Can They be Measured?', *Social Science Information (1967)*, 44(4), pp. 695–729.

Schielke, S. (2008) 'Boredom and Despair in Rural Egypt', *Contemporary Islam*, 2(3), pp. 251–70.

Schopenhauer, A. (1969) *The World as Will and Representation*. Translated by E. F. J. Payne. New York: Dover.

Schutz, A. (1954) 'Concept and Theory Formation in the Social Sciences', *The Journal of Philosophy*, 51(9), pp. 257–73.

Shih, G. (2020) 'Concern –and Boredom– Mount for Those Trapped at Center of the Coronavirus Outbreak', *The Washington Post*, 28 January. www .washingtonpost.com/world/asia_pacific/concern–and–boredom–mount-for-those-trapped-at-the-epicenter-of-the-coronavirus-outbreak/2020/01/28/ 7683fe94-41bd-11ea-99c7-1dfd4241a2fe_story.html (Accessed: 24 May 2020).

Shinkle, E. (2015) 'Alberto García-Alix: Un Horizonte Falso', 17 November. https://americansuburbx.com/2015/11/alberto-garcia-alix-un-horizonte-falso.html (Accessed: 17 December 2020).

Simmel, G. (1995) 'Die Großstädte und das Geistesleben', in R. Kramme, A. Rammsted and O. Rammsted (eds.) *Aufsätze und Abhandlungen 1901– 1908*. Frankfurt am Main: Suhrkamp, pp. 116–131.

Simmel, G. (2002) 'The Metropolis and Mental Life', in G. Bridge and S. Watson (eds.) *The Blackwell City Reader*. Oxford: Blackwell, pp. 11–19.

Simmel, G. (2004) *The Philosophy of Money*. 3rd ed. Edited by D. Frisby. Translated by T. Bottomore and D. Frisby. London: Routledge.

Smit, H. (2014) *The Social Evolution of Human Nature: From Biology to Language*. Cambridge: Cambridge University Press.

Smith, M. (1942) 'The Human Factor in Production', *Nature*, 150(3796), pp. 142–4.

Sobrino, F. (1734) *Dicionario nuevo de las lenguas española y francesa*. 3rd ed. Brussels: Francisco Foppens.

Sommers, J. and Vodanovich, S. J. (2000) 'Boredom Proneness: Its Relationship to Psychological- and Physical- Health Symptoms', *Journal of Clinical Psychology*, 56(1), pp. 149–55.

Sontag, S. (1966) 'One Culture and the New Sensibility', in *Against Interpretation and Other Essays*. New York: Farrar, Straus, Giroux, pp. 293–304.

Spacks, P. A. M. (1995) *Boredom: The Literary History of a State of Mind*. Chicago, IL: University of Chicago Press.

Spaeth, M., Weichold, K. and Silbereisen, R. K. (2015) 'The Development of Leisure Boredom in Early Adolescence: Predictors and Longitudinal Associations with Delinquency and Depression', *Developmental Psychology*, 51(10), pp. 1380–94.

Starobinski, J. (1973) 'The Man Who Told Secrets', *The New York Review of Books*, 22 March, pp. 18–21.

Subirats, E. (2005) 'Postmodern Modernity, or the Transition as Spectacle', *España Contemporánea: Revista de Literatura y Cultura*, 18(2), pp. 31–46.

Svendsen, L. (2005) *A Philosophy of Boredom*. Translated by J. Irons. London: Reaktion Books.

Tardieu, É. (1900) 'L'ennui: Étude psychologique', *Revue Philosophique de la France et de l'Étranger*, 49, pp. 1–30.

Thackray, R. I. (1981) 'The Stress of Boredom and Monotony: A Consideration of the Evidence', *Psychosomatic Medicine*, 43(2), pp. 165–76.

Tolstoy, L. (2016) *Anna Karenina*. Translated by R. Bartlett. Oxford: Oxford University Press.

Toohey, P. (2011) *Boredom: A Lively History*. New Haven, CT: Yale University Press.

Tzara, T. (1981) *Seven Dada Manifestos and Lampisteries*. Translated by B. Wright. New York: Riverrun Press.

Usó, J. C. (2015) *¿Nos matan con heroína? Sobre la intoxicación farmacológica como arma de Estado*. Bilbao: Libros crudos.

Van Tilburg, W. A. P. and Igou, E. R. (2016) 'Going to Political Extremes in Response to Boredom', *European Journal of Social Psychology*, 46(6), pp. 687–99.

Vanderbruggen, N., Matthys, F., Van Laere, S. *et al.* (2020) 'Self-Reported Alcohol, Tobacco, and Cannabis Use during COVID-19 Lockdown Measures: Results from a Web-Based Survey', *European Addiction Research*, 26, pp. 1–7.

Vessey, D. (2009) 'Gadamer and the Fusion of Horizons', *International Journal of Philosophical Studies*, 17(4), pp. 531–42.

Vicens, M. (2014) 'Pasiones prohibidas: lectoras: Lectoras, consumo y periodismo en la Argentina de 1880', *Badebec*, 4(7), pp. 85–108.

Vidal-Folch, I. (1997) *Amigos que no he vuelto a ver*. Barcelona: Anagrama.

Vives, J. L. (1529a) *A very frutefull and pleasant boke called the Instruction of a Christen woman made fyrst in Laten, and dedicated vnto the quenes good grace, by the right famous clerke mayster Lewes Uiues*. Translated by R. Hyrde. London: Thomas Berthelet.

Vives, J. L. (1529b) *Instructión de la muger christiana, agora nuevamente corregido y emendado y reducido en buen estilo castellano*. Translated by J. Justiniano. Alcalá: Miguel de Eguía.

Vives, J. L. (1579) *Institution de la femme chrestienne, tant en son enfance, comme en Mariage & Viduité, avec l'office du mari*. Translated by A. Tiron. Antwerp: Christophe Plantin.

Vives, J. L. (2000) *The Education of a Christian Woman: A Sixteenth Century Manual*. Edited and translated by C. Fantazzi. Chicago, IL: University of Chicago Press.

Vives, J. L. (2002) *The Instruction of a Christen Woman (1529)*. Edited by V. W. Beauchamp, E. H. Hageman, and M. Mikesell. Translated by R. Hyrde. Urbana, IL: University of Illinois.

Vodanovich, S. J. (2003) 'Psychometric Measures of Boredom: A Review of the Literature', *Journal of Psychology*, 137(6), pp. 569–601.

Vodanovich, S. J. and Watt, J. D. (2016) 'Self-Report Measures of Boredom: An Updated Review of the Literature', *The Journal of Psychology*, 150(2), pp. 196–228.

Wangh, M. (1975) 'Boredom in Psychoanalytic Perspective', *Social Research*, 42(3), pp. 538–50.

Watt, J. D. and Ewing, J. E. (1996) 'Toward the Development and Validation of a Measure of Sexual Boredom', *The Journal of Sex Research*, 33(1), pp. 57–66.

Weybright, E. H., Caldwell, L. L., Ram, N., Smith, E. A. and Wegner, L. (2015) 'Boredom Prone or Nothing to Do? Distinguishing between State and Trait Leisure Boredom and Its Association with Substance Use in South African Adolescents', *Leisure Sciences*, 37(4), pp. 311–31.

Wheeler, D. (2020) *Following Franco: Spanish Culture and Politics in Transition*. Manchester: Manchester University Press.

Wilson, C. (1972) *New Pathways in Psychology: Maslow and the Post-Freudian Revolution*. London: Gollanz.

Wittgenstein, L. (1958) *Philosophische Untersuchungen/ Philosophical Investigations*. 2nd ed. Translated by G. E. M. Anscombe. Oxford: Blackwell.

Wittgenstein, L. (1980) *Remarks on the Philosophy of Psychology*. Edited by G. H. von Wright and H. Nyman. Translated by C. G. Luckhardt and M. A. E. Aue. Oxford: Blackwell.

Woolf, V. (1977) *The Diary of Virginia Woolf* (5 vol). Edited by A. O. Bell and Q. Bell. New York: Harcourt.

A Southern Faunist (1801) 'Yeomen of the Last and of the Present Generation', *Gentleman's Magazine and Historical Chronicle*, 71, pp. 587–9.

Zola, É. (1880) *Nana*. Paris: G. Charpentier.

Zola, É. (1922) *Nana*. Translated by B. Rascoe. New York: Alfred A. Knopf.

Zuckerman, M. (1979) *Sensation Seeking: Beyond the Optimal Level of Arousal*. Hillsdale, NJ: Erlbaum.

Acknowledgements

The research for this Element and its availability as Open Access was made possible through Wellcome Trust Collaborative Award no. 108727/Z/15/Z, 'Living with Feeling: Emotional Health in History, Philosophy, and Experience'.

I dedicate this writing to Natalia, from whom I learn to listen.

Cambridge Elements ☰

Histories of Emotions and the Senses

Series Editors

Rob Boddice
Academy of Finland

Rob Boddice (PhD, FRHistS) is Senior Research Fellow at the Academy of Finland Centre of Excellence in the History of Experiences. He is the author/editor of 13 books, including *Knowing Pain: A History of Sensation, Emotion and Experience* (Polity Press, 2023), *Humane Professions: The Defence of Experimental Medicine, 1876–1914* (Cambridge University Press, 2021) and *A History of Feelings* (Reaktion, 2019).

Piroska Nagy
Université du Québec à Montréal (UQAM)

Piroska Nagy is Professor of Medieval History at the Université du Québec à Montréal (UQAM) and initiated the first research program in French on the history of emotions. She is the author or editor of 14 volumes, including *Le Don des larmes au Moyen Âge* (Albin Michel, 2000); *Medieval Sensibilities: A History of Emotions in the Middle Ages*, with Damien Boquet (Polity, 2018); and *Histoire des émotions collectives: Épistémologie, émergences, expériences*, with D. Boquet and L. Zanetti Domingues (Classiques Garnier, 2022).

Mark Smith
University of South Carolina.

Mark Smith (PhD, FRHistS) is Carolina Distinguished Professor of History and Director of the Institutefor Southern Studies at the University of South Carolina. He is author or editor of over a dozen books and his work has been translated into Chinese, Korean, Danish, German, and Spanish. He has lectured in Europe, throughout the United States, Australia, and China and his work has been featured in the *New York Times*, the *London Times*, the *Washington Post*, and the *Wall Street Journal*. He serves on the US Commission for Civil Rights.

About the Series

Born of the emotional and sensory "turns," Elements in Histories of Emotions and the Senses move one of the fastest-growing interdisciplinary fields forward. The series is aimed at scholars across the humanities, social sciences, and life sciences, embracing insights from a diverse range of disciplines, from neuroscience to art history and economics. Chronologically and regionally broad, encompassing global, transnational, and deep history, it concerns such topics as affect theory, intersensoriality, embodiment, human-animal relations, and distributed cognition.

Cambridge Elements ≡

Histories of Emotions and the Senses

A full series listing is available at: www.cambridge.org/EHES

Printed in the United States
by Baker & Taylor Publisher Services